JOY LOVE

BE SELFISH
GIVE TO OTHERS

TAKE THE FIRST STEP TOWARDS
YOUR OWN HAPPINESS

Copyright © 2020 by Joy Love Goodwill

All rights reserved. This book or any portion thereof may not be reproduced or used in any manner whatsoever without the express written permission of the publisher except for the use of brief quotations in a book review.

This cover has been designed using resources from *Freepik.com*

Internal layout designer Dragan Bilic @Upwork

CONTENTS

INTRODUCTION

No one is useless in this world, who lightens the burdens of another.

—Charles Dickens

Being selfish and giving to others may seem like a complete contradiction, but actually it isn't. When you stop to think about it, you'll realise that you often do just that in everyday situations. If your partner is ill, for example; you take care of them and wish for them to recover quickly. Part of this wish comes from pure feelings of love and care for our loved one. And the other part is a selfish wish for them to get better because we'd like our partner to entertain us and give us some attention too, but now all the focus is on them. At times like this we'll put a lot of time and energy into helping our partner to get well, so we can return to normal and get some attention again ourselves. If we're really honest about it, we'll see that our motives in helping our loved ones to get well are partly selfish.

Another example could involve a close friend who is out of work and hard up. Because we care about them, we want them to find a job as soon as possible. Again, part of that feeling is a pure wish for our friend to find a job for their own benefit, but other part is motivated by our selfish desire for them to have enough money to go out with us again; and also because we're a little tired of their continual complaints about the situation. So we encourage them and try to help them get a job if we can, so everything can get back to normal and we'll both feel happier.

When we call someone selfish, it's nearly always meant in a negative sense. We don't believe that such a person is good. But if we look more closely at our own actions throughout the day that we think are good, we'll discover there's usually something in it for us. There's nothing wrong with that so long as we don't have any strong expectations of getting something back, and don't feel angry when nothing materialises. We just need to open our eyes and see the bigger picture. Giving to others can benefit us in ways we might never have expected. We don't need to receive any tangible reward for giving to others. Instead, the act of giving itself can make us happy.

Drug addicts spend a lot of money as well as risking their health and even their life, not to mention endangering their relationships with family and friends. They do all that just for a small glimmer of temporary happiness. Once someone is addicted to a chemical substance, it leads to many problems, and their reality becomes further and further removed from the happiness the drug promised at first. In fact, we all have a natural ability to get high from the chemicals produced naturally within our body. One example is with the 'Helpers High'. This can also be addictive, but once we're aware of its side effects, we'll know how to avoid them so we won't risk our lives by an overdose of goodness. We can help others, get high and feel the happiness we wish for. The best part of it is that we don't have to give very much to feel happy. A small act of kindness will give us a Helpers High in any situation. Although the time we feel high and happy might be short, the effect will linger for much longer.

In this book we'll first look at the idea of motivation. Why should we be more giving? Why should we develop stronger connections to other people and to all other living beings, as well as to our planet? The world is not as friendly and safe as it used to be, but we can change it for the better. Here, we'll look at the selfish reasons for helping others and for giving whatever we can, and doing it willingly. You'll be surprised at the benefits we gain in giving to others. And the best thing about it is that we need selfish reasons to motivate our kind actions only in the beginning. When we see and experience the benefits of our actions and the boost to our happiness level, we'll want to help others more and more. This good habit will become second nature to us before long, and we'll no longer need selfish reasons for our kind actions but will do them purely for the benefit of others. At that point, we'll want to share our delight with everyone. So, be selfish – give to others!

EVOLUTION OF SHARING

It's not how much we give but how much love we put into giving.

—Mother Teresa

Since ancient times, people have lived in communities, sharing and helping each other in every situation. Even though we now have a strong sense of possessiveness and determine which things are 'ours', we still have a sense of community and a strong need to belong to a group. Within the group, whether it's our immediate or extended family, a group of friends, colleagues or a group of people with the same interests or hobbies; we tend to share things with the others. As well as helping and supporting one another, we also like to give gifts, either with or without an occasion.

In any group, you'll find that some members are stronger than others. The stronger ones generally unite to help and support the weaker ones, and once the weaker ones have become stronger, they also help. It's clear that people in a community like to help each other; whether we look at it from the perspective of a micro-community like a family, where parents help their kids, and they in turn help their parents when they grow up. A country can also be viewed from a similar perspective – working people support students and seniors, having received help themselves when they were students and being entitled to assistance when they become seniors. These important traditional values are now changing, however; and it's a little disturbing to see this trend, but humanity still exists, so let's hope it can be preserved. We can contribute by bringing up our children in a moral way by teaching them true values and by giving them a good example.

THE TRADITIONAL COMMUNITY

Traditionally, as I've mentioned, people living in communities shared everything and helped one another in every way. As the African proverb goes 'It takes a whole village to raise a child'; which means that the entire community contributes in one way or another to a child's upbringing for the child to become a decent and well-rounded human being. The older generation shared their wisdom with the younger ones; passing on their life lessons and giving advice. Most members of the community would set an example of the high moral standards to be followed. A young person with a burning question about life would probably turn to the oldest and most respected villager for advice. The villager would take responsibility for guiding them in the right direction, and would wish the youngster well. Members of the community acted rather like to the anonymous support-group workers these days, so that no one would have been left alone in days of trouble. The strong sense of community in former periods meant that people were usually very generous, both with their time and resources. Instead of thinking 'it's mine; I'm keeping it for myself', they gave freely to help someone in need without even thinking about it.

You've probably heard of how people in villages used to keep their house doors unlocked, feeling trust in their community. The thought that someone might come in to steal something didn't even cross their mind. People from different households could borrow things from each other and return them later without any problem. Neighbours took meals and treats to each other as well as sharing recipes and cooking advice. Big celebrations like weddings involved the whole village, and everyone contributed as much as they could; providing tables and chairs, plates and glasses, meals or labour. Everyone was involved and everyone shared the joy together. If someone's house burned down, everyone in the village would rush to help and would invite the unfortunate family into their home to stay. All the men in the community would help to rebuild the family home, while the women would take care of the children and take meals to the men working on the house. People would chip in with household goods and make sure the family had all the essentials for settling well in their new home. Although the different families were probably not blood relatives, they'd all view each other as members of one large family and would feel the urge to help whenever necessary.

People used to share their feelings of joy, excitement or anticipation as well as grief or sadness. The news of any event in the life of another community member would be common knowledge within a matter of hours, and everyone would react to the occasion in an appropriate way. They would celebrate good news together or all grieve together as the situation demanded. This kind of sharing in the community is like an expanded version of marriage – for better or for worse – except more people are included.

This type of sharing within a community still goes on to a certain extent in some cultures, especially in small villages and in less developed countries. Such a sense of community is very rare now in the western world, particularly in big cities. Modern capitalism seems to have blinded us to what's important. Now, an exaggerated sense of self-importance in individuals, together with greed, and the habit of competing rather than cooperating; are the traits that dominate our society.

THE MODERN COMMUNITY

The word *sharing* has acquired a new meaning these days. Most people now share pictures, videos and jokes on social media, which takes the personal approach out of it. We share information, links and inspirational quotes, but we keep our distance. Wishing to create a 'happy person' image on our social media pages, we post things with lots of smiles even though we might feel heartbroken or sad. What we share is only an image on the surface, while our true feelings never see the light of day, but sink heavily and deeply down within us.

Due to social media, the more individual and personal aspects of our friendships are disappearing. Too often we see a group of friends meeting for dinner and drinks and spending at least half the time on their phones checking new posts instead of chatting to their friends who are present in the flesh. This is sad, because the intimacy that comes from sharing our experiences, stories and laughter with friends is the best antidote for loneliness and depression. Spending time with close friends gives us a powerful boost of positive energy that can sometimes last for years. We all have certain memories of events from years ago that still bring a smile to our face when we remember them. Now, we're wasting this potential. These days, even if we're surrounded by many people, we feel lonely. Many of us have a more important relationship with our phone than with our friends. When we have something important to tell everyone, most of us will simply announce it on social media rather than meet our friends to tell them in person. There's even a special feature on certain social media apps to announce that we've got engaged or married. If you don't use social media much, you probably won't know what's happening with your friends.

Online sharing is quite different from sharing offline. It's usually done more for self-centred reasons than from a desire to help. It's all about getting attention and impressing people – we want to look our best, to show everyone that we have the best holidays, that our social life is amazing and that we're happy all the time. We check every two minutes to see how many likes our photos have got and feel pleased for a short time if the number is high. If you watch the videos on YouTube comparing life *with* and life *without* social media, you'll see which option makes people happier. Real sharing happens when we catch up with friends in person, spending time to share our feelings. That way, we get closer to our friends and strengthen our relationships.

THE NEED

*Love and compassion are necessities, not luxuries.
Without them, humanity cannot survive.*

—Dalai Lama

As technology advances, the level of happiness drops. In this age of connectivity people are feeling lonelier than ever before. It's sad, because it seems that it should be the other way around – the more connected people are; the less lonely they should feel. The only solution to this is love and kindness.

The trouble is that the fast pace of life these days puts more and more pressure on us. The high expectations from our family, partner, friends and boss put us in a race for things that are 'bigger' and 'better', and we never seem to stop. We're trying to reach something that's unreachable because nobody knows how high we should aim, and the expectations keep changing as we go. For many people, competing in this race results in unhappiness and depression. It causes a lot of negative thoughts and feelings that literally do poison peoples' lives. Constant thinking and worrying about money doesn't help to lighten the load of negativity either. The economic climate has now left a lot of people without jobs, and some are even without homes.

Many animals are also losing their homes because of human activities. The world is in a crisis in many senses of the word. Unless we change things soon, this planet will not be a good place to live for much longer. We all need to do as much as we can, even if it's just to avoid inflicting any more damage. We need to share things with others, even if it's just a positive thought or an inspiring teaching. Only our love and kindness can save us all and make this planet a great place to live.

DISCONNECTION AND LONELINESS

Logically, as we've seen, it should make sense that the more channels of communication there are, the more connected people should be, but the opposite is, in fact, the case. In theory, progress in technology should help us to communicate better, but in reality, it leaves us feeling more disconnected every day. Of course communication technology is ideal for long-distance connections to contact people in other countries, and helps us not only to talk to our friends and family, but also to see them in video chats. But for the people around us every day, technology has a negative effect on our communication. People can have hundreds or even thousands of friends or followers on social media, but still feel lonely because they don't have any real communication or perhaps any real connection to these people. The quantity of friends may even seem to be more important than the quality. We might not realise how we've got this the wrong way round until we hit a low point in our life when there's no one to help when we need them.

People used to have a special bond with friends they'd had from childhood. There were so many shared experiences and wonderful memories that could sustain a friendship for life. As children, they shared adventures, both real and imaginary, as well as secrets; invented their own games, and drew pictures in the sand or on the pavement with chalk. Then came their first crush and their biggest fears. These friends shared everything.

You might remember how kids used to spend all their free time with their friends, usually playing outside, and it was difficult for parents to get them back into the house even when it was getting dark. The children just couldn't get enough time to play out, and it would be like that every day. Things are different these days. The kids are not really different per se, but are conditioned differently. Now they spend most of their free time inside, and their best friend is usually some kind of gadget. Even when they do spend time with friends, they simply sit together and play with their own phone or tablet. Many of the members of this generation will probably have no real friends in the future because they won't have created any strong bonds with others in childhood. They'll also be missing any happy childhood memories. You can't get deep and lasting memories from communicating on social media or from the information given on the internet without establishing and grounding it with experience and actually living it. Friends will exist simply as numbers on social media sites. Maybe you shared a joke or video with them at some point. Even those who've benefitted from a conventional child-hood with real friends are now struggling to keep their friendships going in this age of technology. What chance do the poor kids have who never learned what real friendship is? People are feeling lonelier than ever before. We used to meet up with friends to give them 'the news' however big or small it was, and we'd get real reactions, real responses and real feelings. Now we just post our news on social media. A few people leave comments and react to our news with emojis, then forget it. We can also check to see who reacted to our news to know which contacts are still our 'friends'.

We're so wrapped up in our everyday life with work, meetings, tons of emails, to-do lists and the endless requirements in every aspect of our life that we forget all about the important things. Many of us are so involved in our 'busyness' that we find ourselves distanced or even completely cut off from our families. Then, we become lonely and often feel resentment and guilt. Ironically, some people have worked so hard for their family, they've had less and less time to spend with them, and ended up with a result quite different from what they'd intended. There are a lot of lonely single people in the world and it's quite obvious why they feel lonely sometimes. It seems even sadder though when people who are actually in a relationship feel lonely. They have all the possibility and potential to feel loved and happy, but they feel dissatisfied. Instead of sharing and giving love and affection, they share feelings of anger and resentment instead. A couple can live together, sleep in the same bed, see each other every day, dine out and go on holiday together, yet still feel lonely and unloved. All the negative feelings have built up over time and it seems impossible to regain the loving feeling they once had in their hearts. There's always room for love though. Instead of expecting the other person to make us happy, we should actively give our love to them. When we give without any expectations, sooner or later the other person will respond in the same way. You'll probably say 'yes, I was giving and giving, but I didn't get the same back' – the trouble was that you were giving with the expectation of reward. To banish loneliness and give ourselves the chance of happiness in a relationship, we need to give our love without any expectation of returns. That way, the other person can't disappoint us.

Many of us now seem to spend most of our lives feeling quite miserable, and this leads us to keep putting off the essential things until later. We think we'll find peace later in retirement, and just postpone any attempts to work on our relationships. There are so many lonely old people in the world now, and they didn't plan it that way. No one wants to be old and lonely. We all have big dreams and plans, but we often let life events control us instead of actively taking control ourselves. Of course we can't control everything in our lives, but we *can* control our reactions to everything that comes our way, no matter how daunting it is. Unfortunately, most people allow life to get in the way of their dreams, and end up getting old without properly pursuing these dreams. Some seniors are lonely because they don't have families, while many others do have families but hardly ever see them. The children have busy lives; they probably have kids of their own and have no time to visit their parents. They may not even live that far away, but there just seems to be no time for a visit. Perhaps we find time for the odd 15-minute or half-hour visit, maybe to drop off or pick up our kids if our parents take care of them sometimes. Even when there are relatives and everyone has phones to communicate easily, and cars for easy transport, so many old people are lonely because their families have no time for visits. Now special charities arrange for volunteers to visit seniors; often just to keep them company.

In the busy life of the modern world, family values and friendships seem to lose all importance. These family relationships used to be the main focus of everyone's life. Extended families of different generations used to live close by; all helping each other and learning from one another. The seniors used to be the most important and respected members of the family. Everyone turned to them for advice, and all the family took responsibility for caring for them. Those connections between people that involved no technology were real. These days, instead of technology helping us and enhancing our relationships with others, it's replacing the things in life that are real and true.

NEGATIVITY IN THE WORLD

The biggest paradox is that everyone wants to be happy and free from problems. There was probably not even one year though in the history of human kind that was free of wars or at least of conflict in one part of the world or another. How come we all want to be happy and to live in peace but are always fighting over something? Some people say, 'If you want to be happy, just be happy!' because it's only our own perception or our way of viewing the world that makes us happy or unhappy. If we understand the truth of how it's all just in our mind, we can really be happy. Then, no external things or situations can affect us. We'd be happy no matter what, and will stop blaming others and pointing fingers in trying to find the cause of our unhappiness.

There is so much hatred in the world now without any good reason. At some point, someone had the idea of hating other people for some reason, and this idea spread like a virus worldwide in many shapes and forms, breeding more hatred every day. We're now so deeply involved in a cycle of hatred and negativity, without seeing a way out; yet at the same time we say we want love and peace and happiness. People sometimes hate others without even knowing them, without even meeting them and without any logical reason. Our likes and dislikes are usually based on our experiences. Sometimes these are from childhood, even though we may have no conscious memory of any strong likes or dislikes towards certain things or objects. Hatred based on an idea put into our head from someone else is irrational and unreasonable. Even though it never brings anything positive into our lives, we're still very susceptive to it.

People also have a lot of hatred mixed with love towards the people they choose to be with or even towards their parents, who gave them the gift of life. It's strange that we develop the strongest feelings of hate for the people we somehow love and who were the kindest to us. We never have such a strong and continuous hatred towards strangers. It's very sad, but true. Instead of seeing how much good our loved ones have done for us, we focus only on the few negative things we see in them. In many cases it's only our perception of them that's at fault, and they actually didn't do anything wrong, and this makes the situation even sadder. When our hate, mixed with rage and anger, is directed at our partner, for example, who cares about us and really loves us, we don't even notice how passionate love became passionate hate. Obviously, we blame the other person and don't realise how the problem is due to our own hazy perception.

When we behave in a negative or indifferent way at home with our loved ones, most of us go to work in the same frame of mind, and likewise, we bring home all the problems at work. Like a hamster on the wheel, we're stuck in the same old story. And we've been spinning on this wheel for so long that we don't even remember how it all started. Did we first bring home problems from work that put us in a bad mood and led to arguments at home; or did the conflicts at home affect our performance at work, where our bad attitude and constant grumpiness put us in trouble with our boss and co-workers? It's rather like the chicken and the egg. One thing is clear though – if we're unhappy at home, we'll probably be unhappy at work as well. In this case, the only time we have left to be happy is while we're asleep. Being in this kind of rut makes people feel depressed.

Add money problems to this cocktail, and we have a recipe for disaster. Many people are suffering from the effects of the economic crisis; having lost their jobs and homes; some still suffering the after effects of the property boom. Even without economic troubles, people are always worried about money and the lack of it. No sum will ever be enough. When we buy products to satisfy our needs and wants, it's called 'consumer behaviour' in marketing. The problem here is that our needs tend to grow alongside our income and we think that if only we could earn 'x' amount more, we'd be happy. Unfortunately, the 'x' amount doesn't help because we suddenly discover new needs to satisfy, and so on. If you think a large sum of money will make you happy, have a look at some of the rich people around, and try to look beyond all their shiny new stuff to see how happy they are. In most cases they're at least as unhappy as everyone else if not more miserable than others because more money brings more problems. There's always something bigger and better to acquire. As long as we associate our happiness with the things we can get, we'll never be happy.

Only by giving to others can you get what you want – true happiness and joy!

PLANET AT RISK

Human beings are not the only ones who want to be happy. All living beings on this planet have the same wish, although their wishes are less conscious than human beings, but they still want to feel they have everything they need and are out of danger. The same goes for the Earth itself, which is also a living organism that holds all life together according to certain laws. All life forms and systems appear to be well designed and coordinated with each part of the whole system supporting the others, similar to a Swiss watch. If we remove even the smallest screw from the watch, the finely tuned mechanism will not work properly. You probably know, for example, that if a creature even as small as a bee becomes extinct, it'll spell disaster for many other species and plants.

Our planet would function perfectly well without human beings and may actually be much better off without us. The Homo sapiens (Latin: 'wise man') is not so wise after all. Few of us see how the planet is at risk and how we humans are slowly destroying it. The Earth is our home and we should appreciate that we have such good conditions to live in. We'd be very uncomfortable living in the Ice Age, for instance. On the other hand, with the rising sea levels now, we could end up under the water. Now we can see the effects of climate change for ourselves. I remember as a child how the coldest winter months were December, January and February, possibly with a little snow in March; then April was warm most years as the spring season began. Summer lasted from June to August, and in

September we'd start to feel the coolness of autumn. These days there's hardly any snow in December, but there's usually still some snow in March and even in the first part of April. And September tends to still be very summery. The seasons seem to have moved forward by one month.

Human activity is also bringing a lot of animals close to extinction. We need to recognise the effect we have on the natural world and on other living beings to allow other creatures to survive in their natural habitat. All living beings on Earth should live with each other harmoniously. Even if there are animals you don't like; all creatures have an important function within the greater scheme of things, and you'd probably like your children to have a variety of wildlife to see, places to explore, good food to eat and fresh air to breathe. Even if we don't have any kids, wouldn't we want that variety of good things for ourselves and for future generations? We need to take care of our home in a broad sense to enjoy the gift of living in a pleasant and healthy environment.

OBSTACLES TO SHARING (OR LAME EXCUSES)

No one has ever become poor by giving

—Anne Frank

We all seem to know that giving small amounts of money to others won't bankrupt us, but we're often still reluctant to help. Many people feel they'd like to give to others, but plan to give to charities only if they become millionaires. Others are so preoccupied with their own affairs; they have no time to even think about giving to others. Some people are prejudiced at the same time, and would never help certain types of people. Inequality exists in the act of giving as well because many believe that certain people deserve help more than others. These are just a few of the reasons that people look at giving as a secondary activity rather than as a part of everyday life.

MONEY

Money – it's the one thing nearly everyone is striving to attain. In the western world people are dreaming of success, piles of money, big houses, flashy cars, expensive clothes, luxury holidays and all the other things that wealth can bring. Our desire for money is so powerful that most of us sell at least a third of our time just to gain money; sometimes even sacrificing our relationships. Unfortunately, in many cases, all this is just to make ends meet. If we're struggling so much ourselves, it's difficult to even think about giving to others. We may feel that we need help too because we're not financially secure. It seems that nobody is going to rescue us, so why should we rescue anyone else? This preoccupation with our own affairs leaves the ones really in need poor and leaves us poor in our spirits as well.

At the same time, there are so many charities that collect money to help people and animals as well as other causes that it seems difficult to help them all so the conclusion is – 'What's the point of trying to help at all?' 'I can't help everyone' or 'I can't change the world'. We may walk down the street on our way to work every day and see homeless people begging with a cup and musicians with a guitar case open to collect money as they play and entertain passers-by. Meanwhile, charity representatives with buckets encourage us to donate or try to persuade us to sign up for making monthly donations. We also see posters on trains or buses requesting us to save kids, cats or dogs. It's so overwhelming to think of all the people and animals that need help that we get lost under the load of information about all the problems and charities, so we don't even know where to start. After all, if we start giving to everyone who asks, we'll soon need help ourselves.

The other issue when it comes to giving money is in not knowing or having any control over how the money will be used. In the case of giving to a homeless person on the street, we're concerned that the money might go on alcohol or drugs rather than on the food that was requested. This thought sometimes stops people from giving money at all. At the same time, we've all heard stories about the misuse of funds within charities. In one recent scandal, a charity head embezzled $20,000 for a painting. Stories like this naturally lead to doubts about the honesty of some charity organisations. Anyone who has regularly supported such charities will feel like a victim who was duped and lost their hard-earned cash.

When giving money to a homeless person, a musician or a charity though, we shouldn't concern ourselves too much about what the money is spent on. Once we've made the decision and made a donation, the recipient is free to decide how to spend it. If the funds are misused, it's a matter that is on the conscience of those who misused it. We can't control everything, nor should we. At least our conscience is clear and we have done a good deed for a day, and feel happy about it.

TIME

Another reason people give for not giving to others is 'I have no time'. We're so preoccupied and so focused on ourselves that we can't spare even a few minutes for something that seems unnecessary just now. How many of us would stop to help somebody on the street? These days, people are so focused on their mobiles and other devices; they seem to deliberately hide behind the technology to avoid any interactions with others. Unless something extraordinary or very startling occurs, most people, not even noticing, would simply pass by someone in need of help. Others might notice but choose to pass by anyway. A certain TV programme shows how people react to certain situations, as a kind of social experiment, and it's interesting to see. It shows teenagers bullying a fat lady, for example; and a child who is lost and crying in the street. Some passers-by stop and look for a few seconds but don't intervene. Others help because they've seen previous episodes of the programme that have inspired them to act. Most of the people who intervene are genuinely concerned, worried and disgusted by the things they're witnessing. Some faith in humanity is restored in seeing this, as many people do stop to help without thought of any possible danger, of uncomfortable feelings or of losing their time. Seeing someone in trouble, they offer to help. Even though it's encouraging to know that many people will not hesitate to help, it's shocking at the same time to see how many others just quickly walk by without even looking or slowing down to evaluate the situation. Are we so busy that we have no time to consider anyone except ourselves?

PREJUDICE

Most of us are prejudiced to some extent, whether we like to admit it or not. More social experiments, this time on YouTube, show situations such as a well-dressed man acting as though ill, then collapsing on the street. Several people immediately rush to help, and one calls for an ambulance. When the same scene is played out with a man appearing to be homeless, not even the people who pass by close to him stop when he collapses. Some people look with disgust as they walk past. It takes a while before someone comes up to help. What if the situation had been real and the person had died after no one had come to help? How would you feel if you'd been the one who'd walked past and later heard the news of how that homeless person had died from a heart attack in a crowded place because nobody had bothered to help and call an ambulance? Unfortunately, situations like this have actually happened in real life.

What if a good looking young woman asked you for help? Would you help? What if the same young woman was plastered with make-up and dressed in a vulgar way as well as having a black eye? Would you help her or would you assume she was a prostitute and stay away?

We live in a modern world and in a multicultural society, but unfortunately things like racism, sexism, Nazism, islamophobia and homophobia still exist. Why is it so difficult for us to put ourselves in the shoes of someone else? What if you became homeless? How would you feel if you were treated like that? Why don't we ask ourselves this question? No one is immune to disaster. We don't know how our lives will turn out. There are a lot of very clever people who thought their life would be brilliant, but who became homeless after some unfortunate event or illness. A proverb in Eastern European countries says that we should never discriminate due to disease, prison or home-lessness because these things can happen to anyone, no matter how clever, good, educated or beautiful they are. Why is it so difficult for us to have compassion and understanding? We could have been born into a different family, a different country or a different time. Would we still be racist if we were born black? Would we still be Islamophobic if we were born and raised in a Muslim family? Would we still be sexist if we were born as a woman? Why can't we see the human being behind the appearance? Imagining that we or someone we love could be in a similar situation, and by nurturing a little compassion, we could easily overcome this problem.

INEQUALITY

For some reason people tend to think that some lives matter more than others. You might say 'No, it's not true', but just think about it. Following a big terror-ist attack in France, millions of people changed their profile picture on Facebook to express their support for France. A much bigger terrorist attack in Turkey with more victims resulted in a much weaker reaction, however. Do people think that European's lives matter more than people's lives in the Middle East?

And inequality is not only about race, gender, sexual orientation, age, social status or even looks. Inequality exists when we compare the lives of humans and the lives of animals. Animals can become vulnerable due to the destructive actions of humans. And nearly everyone will remember the wave of disgust after seeing pictures posted of hunters posing with their prey and showing their pride in killing an animal. If we're not helping animals we should at least not hurt them.

We should practice thinking that all lives are equal and they all matter. We need to develop a feeling of compassion and try to understand the situation from another's perspective. We never know when we'll need help ourselves and when we'll be praying for the kindness of others. In a difficult situation we would hope for compassion and care from others, so we should start spreading kindness now by giving to others.

WE'RE ALL LIVING BEINGS ON ONE PLANET

All living creatures are connected, and we all share the Earth as our home. Instead of fighting with each other and being ready to cut each other's throats just to gain some advantage, we should live in peace and understand the meaning of community. Having a sense of community reduces the feelings of loneliness and helplessness, and brings help, hope and happiness instead. Taking care only of ourselves is ignorant. We need to look at the bigger picture. Our planet is our home and so our life and future depend entirely on the health of the Earth. We need to take better care of our home if we want to live long and prosperous lives. We shouldn't underestimate the importance of all living creatures because they're all here for a reason; all to take part in the harmonious existence of this planet. One simple example comes by just googling, 'What would happen if bees were extinct?' Do you think humans are more important than bees? Well, think again. The Earth would thrive without humans (the way they act now), but would suffer an existential crisis without bees. People need to address global warming and pay more attention to sustainable living and natural energy sources more if they want to live healthy and happily. By making efforts to protect the planet we are technically giving to ourselves and contributing to our own wellbeing. In this matter, it is again, good to be selfish!

MOTIVATION BEHIND GIVING

If you want others to be happy, practice compassion. If you want to be happy, practice compassion.

—Dalai Lama

For any action we take in life a motive lies behind it. Some motives are very clear, but for others that are difficult to recognise, we need to take a closer look and analyse the situation. The motivation behind giving to others can be a genuine wish to help or there can be a hidden agenda. Nevertheless, help is help whatever the reason behind it.

GENUINE WISH TO HELP OTHERS

There are different levels of giving to others. Some people want to give so long as it doesn't hurt them. Others are happy to help even if it costs them a substantial amount of time or money. And the highest level of giving to others is when someone sacrifices something precious or something that is very important to them in order to help another person.

Whichever level of giving it is, the best motivation behind it is the genuine wish to help others. People who provide help to others have no expectations whatsoever of getting anything back. They help just because they can; they have compassion and want to help. These genuine givers act selflessly as they require no reward, although in some cases they might receive some kind of reward afterwards for a heroic act such as saving somebody's life, but the reward was never the initial goal or motivation for them to help.

Every day, people give to others, sometimes heroically or just in giving little things and showing concern for the well-being of others. Most of these acts go completely unnoticed, but that doesn't matter at all to the genuine givers. Some of the small things we take for granted and don't even consider as acts of kindness are often overlooked and underappreciated. We wouldn't want to imagine the world without those little things though. For example, teenagers giving up their seat to an elderly person or a pregnant woman; or a mother washing her children's clothes or preparing costumes for a kids' play are simple acts of kindness we take for granted. Imagine a world where no one did those things and simply took care of themselves as individuals. It would be a scary place to live. In general, mothers are probably the most genuine, selfless givers who'll always put their child's interests above their own. Unfortunately, mothers are the most underappreciated people in the world because we take them so much for granted and only start appreciating their kindness and care when we get older and have our own kids.

Sometimes we feel sorry for others and that's why we help them. Sometimes we want to help others because we want them to be happy or at least we want to cheer them up if only for a short moment, and the smile on their face or joyful tear in their eye is the best reward we could get. No returned favour or gift is necessary because even the smallest glimpse of joy for one second on the other person's face is all we really need. It's amazing how a small act of kindness can instantly add to happiness so that both the giver and receiver are uplifted.

SELFISH MOTIVES

Giving to others is good, but there are sometimes hidden motives and agendas. It's not a form of barter based on 'you scratch my back and I'll scratch yours' because this is simply an exchange of favours; where someone pays for a future favour with a present one. That's just a simple transaction like an exchange of goods. The type of giving that involves selfish ulterior motives can also be done to gain popularity. Trying to help others for this reason has recently become a trend on YouTube where people post videos of themselves trying to help homeless people. They do this to get more viewers, likes and shares. It looks as though they use homeless people almost as props in their videos without much thought for these people's feelings. The videos show them giving money or food to homeless people and sometimes bragging about it as if they're heroic; then asking you to subscribe to their YouTube channel.

There's no doubt that helping homeless people in any way at all is much better than doing nothing. And trying to gain popularity and ratings this way is much more valuable than throwing a backpack at someone and posting it (I'll probably never understand the point of 'Backpack Challenge'). At least helping homeless people to gain popularity actually has some kind of positive effect and might inspire others to do the same. When the wish to help is genuine, the only selfish motive of helping is the good feeling it gives inside.

GENUINE OR NOT, IT'S BETTER THAN NOTHING

Whether the motivation behind giving stems from a genuine wish to help or from a selfish wish to show off and gain popularity, the result is still positive for the recipient. When the help is genuine; it's more rewarding, both in the feelings and in the uplifted energy levels for both the giver and receiver, but the help given still counts otherwise. It's like a stepping stone towards an ideal world where people help others without any expectation of reward. We can't expect everyone to have kind hearts and become altruists overnight though. Humanity needs to go through a long process of change, and we all have to start somewhere. A bodybuilder can't expect to get a six-pack straight away; it needs exercise, healthy eating and time. Likewise, you can't start from doing 100 sit-ups a day if you've never exercised before. You'll injure yourself, burn out very quickly and be unlikely to reach your goal. The process has to be slow and steady; starting from maybe just 5 sit-ups a day and increasing to 10 sit-ups a day after a week. After 3 months, 100 sit-ups won't hurt in the slightest because you'll have gradually trained and prepared your body for it. The same applies to many things in life. No one becomes a master at something the first time they try it.

Humanity needs to take this knowledge and apply it in developing compassion and kindness in our hearts. We need to train ourselves and gradually, our thoughtful actions will fulfil us, and the world will become a better place. You might say 'Yes, but not everyone will become good and people will still behave badly.' True, but people don't like to stand out from the crowd too much; and most people feel more comfortable doing what the others do because they want to be accepted by the group. Imagine if showing compassion was standard behaviour, anyone who was not compassionate would feel out of place. They'd eventually adopt kind and compassionate behaviour as well. It will take more time for some people than for others as everyone is different. Even if some don't become kind-hearted, any increase in people starting to act compassionately is still progress.

BE SELFISH – GIVE TO OTHERS

When we feel love and kindness toward others, it not only makes others feel loved and cared for, but it helps us also to develop inner happiness and peace.

—Dalai Lama

Altruism is described as a 'disinterested and selfless concern for the well-being of others' when someone presents a gift or donation to a recipient – another person, an animal or a cause. However, according to many researches, the giver actually receives more from the act of kindness than the receiver. So the idea that altruism is a selfless act to benefit others is not entirely true. The helper gets a lot of intangible benefits that include feeling happier and more satisfied with life as well as better physical health and a feeling of gratitude.

HELPER'S HIGH

The warm feeling we have in our heart after helping someone is due to the endorphins released into our brain as a result. It has a similar effect to exercise.

These hormones are our natural pain and stress killers and help us to come out of a bad mood or depression. This positive energy that comes from helping others makes us feel happier and activates areas of the brain identified with pleasure, social interaction and trust. We often think that spending money on ourselves will cheer us up, but studies actually show quite different results. We feel happier by giving money to someone else. This experience encourages us to perform small acts of kindness every day because it lifts our happiness levels in ways we couldn't predict or imagine.

Have you ever seen a really angry volunteer who willingly helped someone and got a thankful look and maybe a hug from the recipient? Probably not? When we have a warm feeling in our heart and we want to give to someone, whatever it is we're willing to give; we feel joy and satisfaction and all sorts of pleasant emotions. A smile naturally lights up our face and we feel great. Nobody is asking you to give all you have or more than you feel comfortable about giving. In other words, it's best to give what you can without any feeling of loss. It can be as simple as a big smile or a hug. You'd be surprised at how small things done in the right place at the right time can have a much greater effect than big things in the wrong situation and at the wrong time. For example, a bottle of water for a thirsty person stuck in the desert is a priceless gift; whereas a gold bar is of little use in that situation. Taken out of the context, the gold will appear as a much better and more valuable gift, but genuine help means understanding and giving the person what they need if we can. With a simple act of kindness we can achieve triple results – the recipient will be happy; we'll feel happy and enjoy feeling the Helper's High; and most likely the recipient will help someone else in the future as a result; creating a ripple effect. If everyone was open to helping others as much as possible and without any feeling of loss, the whole world would be high on happiness and smiles would follow us wherever we went.

FORGETTING OUR PROBLEMS

When we focus on helping someone else we tend to forget about our own problems. This can be very easily explained – our problems exist only in our mind. Once we focus on something outside ourselves, we forget about our own troubles because we can't fully focus on two things at the same time. Let's say we're cooking our dinner, and thinking about some problem we think we have, going over it again and again in our mind. We feel sorry for ourselves and don't see any solution. The problem can become over-whelming and seem like the most important thing in the world. A small distraction is all it takes for it to disappear, however. It doesn't matter whether the distraction is something pleasant or not, it works in the same way. It could be an unexpected phone call from a good friend we haven't spoken to for ages that cheers us up, or alternatively, our dinner might get burned in the oven, setting off the fire alarm and filling the kitchen with smoke. The effect is the same – our problem just disappears. Our mind then returns to it after the distraction is gone. But if we consider what happened here, we could learn how to dispose of all our problems, as we see them, in one very simple step – by redirecting our thoughts towards something else, preferably something positive. This doesn't mean evading our responsibilities such as paying bills, for example; but means being honest with ourselves and seeing our problems for what they are – the result of us making a mountain out of a molehill in our mind. When we shift our focus away from ourselves and on to others, we automatically forget our problems and they cease to exist.

GRATITUDE FOR WHAT WE HAVE

We all know that a feeling of gratitude makes us feel better and more positive about our lives. We feel uplifted and energised when we spend a few minutes every day considering the reasons we should feel grateful, either in our minds or by writing them down. This practice has the amazing power to change our perspective on our life and helps to dispel most of our problems. When we're grateful for what we have, it's difficult to be unhappy about what we don't have. This doesn't mean that we shouldn't strive for better things; it simply means that we can achieve them with a happy mind. It means the journey will be much more pleasant and smooth because positive thoughts attract positive things.

Although we might naturally feel grateful for everything we have, we may, nonetheless, sometimes start to think 'the grass is greener on the other side' and feel we lack something. That's the moment when unpleasant feelings start to appear. Helping less fortunate people starts to open our eyes and shows us how the grass in our own garden is really very green; putting everything into perspective for us. When we see the problems other people are facing we suddenly realise how fortunate we are and how grateful we should be for everything we have. Having a sense of appreciation and gratitude is essential to our happiness and can inspire us to help others who are less fortunate.

HELPING IS GOOD FOR YOUR PHYSICAL HEALTH

Many researches show the positive effect that giving, helping and supporting others has on our physical health. Studies over a five-year period of elderly people who volunteer and support others show they're less likely to die in that time than the ones who don't volunteer. One of the main reasons that giving to others is linked to a longer lifespan and better physical health is that it decreases stress levels. As already mentioned, helping others releases endorphins, which are natural pain and stress killers. And we all know that stress can cause all sorts of diseases from mild discomfort in our stomach to serious illnesses. This is just one more proof that we should help others at least for our own sakes if we're not feeling generous enough to do it for the benefit of others.

HELPING ENHANCES OUR SOCIAL LIFE AND MENTAL HEALTH

Human beings need to feel a connection to others in order to feel happy. That's why we always create different kinds of groups in order to regularly meet up with others. We like to find others with similar interests to share our common interests. Besides the benefits mentioned above, volunteering and helping others also allows us to belong to a group of like-minded people with similar goals. When we help others, we create a strong bond with them; we feel closer to them and they feel closer to us. We can often find new friends or maybe even fall in love by taking part in charitable groups and events. We expand our social circle at the same time, and increase the number of positive and interesting interactions with those around us. Also, studies show that when we give, we're far more likely to get something back, whether from the receiver or someone else. An abundance of love and kindness is created, and the positive energy that flows in this environment makes us feel happier and enriches our lives.

TYPES OF RECIPIENTS

As we work to create light for others, we naturally light our own way.

—Mary Anne Radmacher

Giving to your child, friend, colleague or family member is different from giving to a stranger. We can easily find kindness in our heart to give to someone we love, but giving to strangers doesn't come so naturally. On the other hand, giving to strangers is probably easier than giving to someone we know but really dislike or even hate. We should be more selfish in this situation and try to free ourselves from hatred because it doesn't benefit us or anyone else. We need to cherish ourselves and stop hating people because the only person who is really damaged that way is the one who hates. The people we hate might not even know we hate them so there's no negative impact for them. Finding compassion and kindness in our hearts to give and help others should extend to everyone.

GIVING TO THE ONES WE LOVE

Giving to benefit the people we love is something we don't think much about because it comes so naturally to us. When we have deep feelings for someone we're closely connected to, caring about them with all our heart, we may not even view our actions towards them as 'giving'. In our wish to make the other person happy, we spare no time or effort in doing everything we can to bring a smile to their face. The same is true with the pets we love and take care of; feeding them, petting them, taking them for walks, bathing them and playing with them.

We really worry, if the ones we love have some kind of problem. We worry if they get injured or ill or if they feel sad, or literally if anything out of ordinary happens to them to affect their well-being. We don't stop to think when we see they need help. Instead, we mobilise all our strength and attention to address the issue and spend however long is necessary to solve any problem. We simply act as our heart dictates.

But even in the process of giving to the ones we love, we usually do have certain expectations, except perhaps when a mother gives to her child, which is probably the purest form of giving. If you've ever known a couple get a divorce, you'll probably have seen how all the unfulfilled expectations spring out with the force of water rushing out from a broken dam. And then the 'blame game' begins with phrases like 'I gave you so much and you gave me nothing!' or 'You're so ungrateful – I gave you all I had!' The strange thing is that both parties usually feel the same way because they're both looking at the issue from their own perspective. It's like two people arguing over which number they see when looking at 6/9 from opposite ends– if we look only from our own perspective it's impossible to see the truth and resolve the differences. Even though giving to the ones we love seems the easiest way of giving, we need to adjust our feelings, expectations and attachments in this process. We should be giving only because we want to share our love and because we want to make the other person happy, not because we hope to get something in return. This attitude comes naturally when both partners have a genuine love for each other. There's no need for selfish motives in this type of giving, but if you sometimes struggle to find motivation in giving to your loved ones, you can use selfish reasons something like these:

Selfish reason 1: *Seeing your loved ones happy will make you feel good too.*

Selfish reason 2: When you have no expectations of getting anything back in return, you have nothing to lose, so you can give to your loved ones with a happy and peaceful heart. You'll have the satisfaction of knowing you've done your best.

Selfish reason 3: It'll feel much better to receive something in return unexpectedly, and this will help you to recognise who has genuine feelings towards you. Your generosity can help you find the right partner. If you're always giving and your partner never reciprocates, it's probably a sign that you should look for someone different who'd love you too.

Selfish reason 4: You'll have a clear conscience, and your generosity will help you at the end of your life. If you believe in karma and possible future lives, your generosity will also reap rewards.

GIVING TO PEOPLE WE KNOW

People we know can include our extended family, colleagues and friends as well as acquaintances such as friends of friends. It could be someone we met on a trip, the person behind the counter in a coffee shop we often go to, the mechanic who fixes our car, someone we met on a course or someone we had a date with. We can connect on different levels with people who are of varying importance to us. It's less about how much time we spend with them than about the quality and strength of the relationship. For example, we might see a colleague every day at work, but we probably care more about our friend who we see only once a month. We're more likely to help someone we know, regardless of how close they are to us and even if we've met the person only once, than help a stranger. Sometimes our inclination to help even extends to the point that we're happy to help a person we actually don't know and have never met before, but who is somehow connected to someone we know. This tendency is especially strong with someone we keep hearing about, as when we actually meet them, we feel we know them already. Even a tenuous connection can transform a stranger into 'someone we know' even though it isn't strictly true.

Giving to people we know is fairly easy. We already have some kind of relationship with that person and can easily show them kindness. Sometimes we might help only because we don't want to cause any bad feelings or even vengeful actions in the future though. We want to avoid hearing words like, 'I remember how you refused to help me when I asked, so I'm not going to help you now'. In this case the expectation to get something in return still exists. We seem to struggle to give to people when we won't get anything in return. Why can't we just give to others with the selfish reason to feeling happy in return?

Don't get me wrong, we shouldn't give everyone everything whenever anyone asks as that would just turn us into a doormat. Likewise, a mother doesn't give her child everything that he or she asks for. If a child asks for a bar of chocolate five minutes before dinner, for example; you know what the answer will probably be. Giving love and care certainly doesn't mean giving someone everything they ask for. So if you're scared that giving to people you know will make you a doormat as people will take advantage of you, just remember the bar of chocolate before dinner example. Use your intelligence and common sense to evaluate the situation. Sometimes refusing to give someone what they ask for actually helps them. If your friend is trying to stop smoking and asks you for a cigarette, refusing them will help. Yes, fair enough, your friend will probably feel angry with you at that moment, but will be grateful in the long run. When it comes to fighting something negative like an addiction, there can be a need for toughness.

If you can't help people you know for selfless reasons, help them for selfish reasons. They'll feel grateful and you'll feel proud of yourself. That's an amazing feeling that will definitely put a smile on your face as you go through the day.

Selfish reason 1: *Wisely helping people you know will make you more lovable and popular; people will respect you, and you'll also have a better chance of receiving help if and when you need it.*

Selfish reason 2: *You can feel proud of yourself for your good deed.*

Selfish reason 3: *Helping someone will make you feel great; it'll uplift your spirit and put a smile on your face, maybe even for the whole day.*

GIVING TO PEOPLE YOU KNOW, BUT DON'T NECESSARILY LIKE

Mmm... this is a tricky one. To be honest, on your path to becoming a more giving, compassionate and kinder person, you can leave this one for the time being. It's very difficult for us to help anyone we dislike because we've stored up grievances and feel resentful. Not only do we have no desire to help, but we can hardly stop ourselves from hurting them back. You probably feel like that about certain people in your life. It could be an annoying colleague, a messy flatmate, an ex-lover who dumped you or anyone else who hurt or annoyed you at some point. But the problem here is that by holding on to negative feelings and resentment, we slowly destroy ourselves and the other person is not affected at all. You can find information online on how hatred and anger affect us socially, psychologically and physically. This happens if we hold on to these negative feelings of hate, and you'll see how harmful it can be. It's sad that so many people are torturing themselves like this on a daily basis.

To turn this situation around, we can start to think about actually helping people we don't particularly like. This can be done in two stages: firstly, by freeing ourselves of negative feelings like hatred and anger, and secondly, by starting to help people we dislike (or used to dislike). Well, the first one should be very easy to accomplish through selfish motivation because you'll feel great once you manage to rid yourself of negative emotions. Your mind will be clear and calm, and you'll feel much happier and more fulfilled. And who among us wouldn't want to be happy? Unfortunately, for some reason, many people choose to be angry rather than happy. We are all in control of what we want to be. If you want to be happy, then be happy. Why do we often leave our happiness in the hands of others and sadly, in many cases, with people who don't really care about us. Be selfish in this sense and be happy for yourself. There are plenty of books or YouTube videos about how to get rid of anger and hatred and start living a positive and happy life. Once you've managed this, the second part of helping people you dislike will be even easier, because, guess what – you don't hate them anymore. So once we've released ourselves from these negative emotions, we'll lose our feelings of dislike for certain people we know, and find it much easier to help them.

If you still think it'll be difficult to forgive and to start helping people you don't like, just think about it from a more selfish point of view. Wouldn't you want to be a unique person who is admired by others? Maybe you don't need to go as far as Mother Teresa, but if you could manage to free yourself from hatred and anger, and learn how to put the needs of others above your own, you'd not only become a much happier person, but you'd also be pretty unique. Probably only 5 percent of all human beings are capable of doing so, and that would make you pretty cool.

Selfish reason 1: Helping others helps us enormously. Learning how to overcome our anger is the best gift we can give ourselves.

Selfish reason 2: You'll gain the respect of others because they'll see you as a very good person who overcomes personal feelings to help others.

Selfish reason 3: *Helping people we dislike will help us to become happier because we'll gain control of our emotions and moods, and won't let any annoying person affect our happiness.*

Selfish reason 4: *Even if the person you dislike won't accept your help, the credit will still be yours as you showed kindness by trying to help, and so the other person will appear to be in the wrong. Even if you really hate someone, it's better to try and overcome this feeling and be generous towards them than show anger and hatred.*

GIVING TO STRANGERS

Although giving to strangers is probably not as difficult as giving to someone you don't like, it's still challenging. We tend to undermine the importance of people we don't know. Although there are many exceptions, and plenty of good Samaritans ready to help, the world would be so much better if such people were more like the rule than the exception. For example, if your car breaks down, you'd want someone to stop and help, and would probably feel quite disappointed if you needed to wait a while. But if we see somebody else in a car that's broken down, we probably don't care much and just pass by. We expect that someone else will stop and help or feel we don't have time, or don't understand much about cars anyway. This attitude reveals the double standards so many of us have, as everything depends on which side of the situation we're on.

Imagine a world where most people consider others, putting themselves in other people's shoes and not hesitating to help when necessary. Together with them, we can create that ideal world. The attitude would be, 'I'll help this person in need because if I were in that situation, I believe someone would help me'. This transformation will not happen overnight but will take one or two generations of actively promoting compassion and kindness as the source of happiness. It's possible to achieve it if we all act together.

So again, be selfish and start the ball rolling towards this happier future. Wouldn't you like your grandchildren to respect you as an active member of the generation that began to make the change towards a better world? Wouldn't you like your kids to have a better life? Wouldn't you like to know they'll get help from strangers when you're not there? A world where people are kind, compassionate, happy and smiling all the time would be an amazing place to live in. If there was a magic box that you could open and take out a pound for yourself and a pound for another person

– how often would you open that box? Well helping others is like using that magic box – it gives you and the other person a happy feeling – and often involves no expense.

Selfish reason 1: *Helping others creates good karma for us, and we send out positive energy to the universe. When the energy is positive, there's more chance that we'll get help ourselves when we need it. It's worth remembering that the reverse is also true, however.*

Selfish reason 2: *Helping another person, even a stranger, will put a smile on the faces of at least two people. The smiles can spread to others who weren't involved but who simply witnessed the act of kindness. Don't we all want to spread joy and feel joy?*

Selfish reason 3: *We'll help to create a better place to live for ourselves and for everyone else.*

GIVING TO THE EARTH

Giving does not only involve other people. Our planet is now at risk, and it's in our power to change the course of self-destruction we're now on. Global warming is real and all scientists agree on that. The politicians that deny global warming are paid to say that by big oil companies. Even though politicians should serve the interests of the people who elected them, in reality they serve the corporations that pay them to protect their multi-billion businesses. As intelligent creatures, we should be able to differentiate between right and wrong. Should we believe: all the scientists with actual proof or the corrupt politicians?

It was admirable that Leonardo DiCaprio drew attention to climate change by presenting the documentary film 'Before the Flood' in 2016. The makers of this movie made it freely accessible to everyone online, to reach as wide an audience as possible. The scientists' warnings about climate change may have fallen on deaf ears for decades but people are now starting to listen, especially through the power of Hollywood. But the message is still being spread too slowly. More celebrities need to back up the scientists in their interviews, speeches and documentaries, and these celebrities should do this more often and more assertively. We could change our habits and slow down global warming; hopefully even reversing the process and healing the planet from the damage already done.

You might say that you don't particularly care about the planet and that you're too insignificant to change anything. In the UK, the supermarket Tesco uses the slogan 'Every little helps', and that is so true. We encounter examples of this principle in our life every day, and we know that any big change or achievement doesn't happen overnight. If you needed to single-handedly prepare a dinner for all the members of a large extended family, you'd be exhausted by the end of the day. But if everyone joined forces, each one doing a small task to help, it would be a case of 'many hands make light work'. Someone would peel the onions, someone else would chop vegetables, one or two would cook and another would serve the dishes; then a few people would help to clean up. You'd probably end up just coordinating everyone and not doing much yourself. Another example is with your grocery shopping – you've probably been in a situation where you get the bill, which comes to, let's say; £32 and feel you've been cheated because you have only a few small items costing one or two pounds. But when you look through the receipt, you see no mistake and feel surprised at how a few small things could add up to £32. Little things soon add up, and this can also work in a positive way – your impact through giving may be small and you alone can't change the world, but it can make a huge difference when many people play their small part. And the difference can be good or bad – it works both ways, so we should choose wisely which way we want to make a change.

Even if you don't want to start giving something to the Earth – be selfish and do it for yourself! Imagine a world where you can never see the sun because of all the smog and pollution in the city. At the same time, you never have a chance to breathe fresh air again either, and need to wear a protective mask. This is not a bad dream or a fantasy – it's already happening in China. Imagine if you went on holiday to the seaside and found the beach and the sea all smelly and full of rubbish. What if there were no forests left to walk in? Skiing would be a thing of the past because the temperatures would be too high for snow. Does anyone want to live in a world that looks like an apocalyptic scene from a horror movie?

Instead of gradually destroying the planet, why not become a small but important part of the change towards saving it, and living in a beautiful and harmonious world? Do it for your own sake. No one is asking you to become an extremist activist fighting for causes and initiating all kinds of protests. But, for example; if you see a petition for a good cause to help save the planet, please stop being passive and sign it. Take a bag with you when you go shopping and reuse it whenever you shop instead of buying a new plastic bag. You'll no longer have piles of plastic bags taking up space in the house and you'll not be adding polluting plastic to the environment. If you're planning to buy a car, buy an electric one – you'll never need to buy petrol again, and you'll be helping to save the environment. Rinse the plastic items for recycling before putting them outside to prevent animals from taking out the plastic or cardboard and make sure these items are collected, and not strewn all over the drive and scattered by the wind.

No one is asking you to become obsessed with climate change and alter your daily habits overnight. It'll be great if you become aware of the issue though and start to think of which small changes you could make in your habits. We are creatures of habit, but we can slowly change our habits step-by-step and by starting small. Also, when you know that people can adapt to change, and can develop a new habit in about 21 days, suddenly the task doesn't seem so difficult. It simply requires you to focus carefully on your actions for a very short time before they become quite natural to you. If you want to enjoy fresh air, sunshine, revitalising walks in the forest, skiing trips or holidays on the beach, then why not play your part? You can google 'small changes to save the environment' and find plenty of tips for simple actions you can start doing from today.

Selfish reason 1: As this planet is our home, we want to live in a clean environment just as we like to live in a clean house. We should take care of our environment.

Selfish reason 2: *We want to breathe clean, fresh air and avoid inhaling toxins from polluted air. Taking care of the environment will help us to keep healthy.*

Selfish reason 3: *We'll enjoy our holidays more, whether we have a beach holiday, a skiing holiday or one involving outdoor activities. Being surrounded by rubbish would spoil everything.*

Selfish reason 4: *Saving the environment and planet will help prevent worsening natural disasters and extreme weather conditions. Everyone wants to live in a safe place without the threat of destructive winds, floods or droughts.*

GIVING TO ANIMALS

Animals in the wild take care of themselves perfectly well in their natural environment, but when people start interfering in animal habitats, the creatures are at risk and we need to act. Some species are on the verge of extinction and the numbers of many others are in very rapid decline and in danger of disappearing from the Earth altogether. Wild animals would be fine without any human help; we just need to stop destroying their habitat and food, as well as stop treating them like trophies. You'll probably say there's nothing you can do to stop this process, but aside from becoming an activist and fighting the big corporations that are causing destruction in one way or another, or chaining yourself to a tree, there are more moderate actions you can consider. You could avoid buying anything made from animal horns or fur, for example; ensure you leave no litter when you visit the countryside or seaside; make sure you extinguish your camp fire and don't toss away a cigarette in the forest without making sure it's completely out. Finally, don't support any form of entertainment that uses animals. You could donate to organisations that plant trees or start an initiative (or sign one, if it already exists) for governments to bring in a law that requires corporations to plant two trees for every single one they cut for their business. In this way you'll help to restore the habitats of birds and animals.

You might not care too much about the animals, and you're probably not a Greenpeace activist or planning to become one, but again – do these things for yourself. Would you want to live in a world with no wild animals left in it? How would you enjoy your safari trip or scuba diving? If you read a story to your kids about Winnie-the-Pooh what will you say when they ask you about the animals in the book? 'This is the bear – an animal that no longer exists because humans destroyed it. The bear's friend is a piglet – the animal we cruelly bred in factory farms and then ate, and then there's the tiger – it's like a big orange cat with black stripes that also became extinct because of humans'. Do you think your kids would still enjoy the story if they knew that cruel humans had destroyed all those wonderful animals from the book in real life? You want the best for yourself and you love your kids (or your future kids) so why not help prevent the extinction of animals so we can all keep the world an interesting and colourful place?

Selfish reasons 1: We enjoy looking at pictures of all the attractive and fascinating animals or going to see them on a safari or in a zoo. We'd lose these pleasures if many animals became extinct.

Selfish reason 2: Saving animal habitats will allow our children and grandchildren to see and appreciate a wide variety of animals.

Selfish reason 3: If we don't preserve the natural environments of animals, some of them will move closer to our homes and it might not be very safe for us with grizzlies wandering the streets.

GIVING TO THE CAUSE

The world we live in is a beautiful place but there are problems within it we need to try and solve. Many different organisations are fighting for a better world and initiating various projects to help achieve this aim. People can contribute to making the world a happier and more harmonious place to live in by choosing from a number of different causes to donate to or support. These include causes such as clean water, education, working against hunger, fighting disease and helping children / the elderly / women etc. There's plenty of choice with over one and a half million charities to choose from in all.

A more difficult question is how to choose the right cause or charity to donate to. Some people might be naturally drawn to one organisation in particular, whereas others will choose one that addresses a problem from their own life experience and situation – where a family member has had some kind of disease or has been homeless at some point, for example. Someone who has a family member or friend with a disease that needs more research will feel motivated to help a charity for this particular cause, not only by donating, but also by spreading information and campaigning. Some people feel so passionate about a cause that they join the organisation as volunteers and help to publicise this cause; contributing a lot of time and effort to it.

Supporting and forwarding a cause can be a very positive experience. Caring about something more than yourself is a very admirable quality that requires both strength and kindness. The idea of sharing with others and putting thought and effort into improving their well-being is now attracting more and more people. It's like a light at the end of the tunnel. It could be that people start to care about others more because they already have everything they need themselves and so they wish to share. The recent popularity of positive-thinking teachings is also encouraging people to give. The biggest factor that has brought such a surge of interest in giving and helping though is the wide-reaching communication now possible through the internet. It's likely that many people wanted to help previously, but often couldn't find the way to do it. The availability of news and ideas from around the world has therefore made charitable causes a lot more accessible to a greater number of people.

The big interest now in helping and giving is very good news. It shows that humanity is slowly moving towards a better world. Maybe you're one of the people who really don't care though because you don't have any serious problems at the moment or don't have any personal attachment to any of the causes that would make you want to donate or help. Here are a few selfish reasons for participating in the process of making the world a better place:

Selfish reason 1: *No one is immune to disease; so you never know when you could be a victim. As you'd probably hope that an effective treatment would be available, donating to charities that research various diseases will help safeguard you and your family for the future, to have the best chance of being happy and healthy.*

Selfish reason 2: *What goes around comes around. You never know what kind of help you might need in the future. If you donate or contribute to making education available for all children, one of them might help you in the future. Maybe one of them will become a doctor and save your life or that of one of your children, or one of them could become a mechanic who'd help when your car breaks down in the middle of nowhere.*

Selfish reason 3: *Making your own contribution will boost your satisfaction and put you in a great mood. Helping others feels good and it lifts the spirit. You might not believe that helping can have such a positive effect, but how do you know if you've never tried it? Why not give it a try? Start by helping three people every day for a week and see how you feel at the end of that time. It'll be very surprising if you don't feel really great. You'll lose very little in any case (you don't have to help with* *money). If you do find that it doesn't work, you could try helping just to boost your own sense of importance and sense of control. Lots of people get high on a feeling of power, so you're bound to enjoy it as well.*

Selfish reason 4: *Everyone is getting older, and the time will come when we could feel lonely, vulnerable and needing help. So helping to create a solid infrastructure to take care of the elderly will help you in the future.*

GIVING TO YOURSELF

'This one is easy' – you'll say. Who doesn't like giving to themselves? Even people who are not very confident love themselves although they might not admit it even to themselves. In fact everyone wants to be happy and to enjoy a feeling of well-being. Doesn't everyone want to be comfortable, well-fed, well-rested and happy? If that's true, then why are there so many unhappy people? Now when you think about it, if we all love ourselves and find it easy to give to ourselves, we should all give ourselves everything we need and be completely happy, always smiling, and never complaining about anything. We'd be content with the money we have, and wouldn't worry even if we had a problem in our lives. We'd sort it out without too much complaint so we could return to our content-ed state as soon as possible, wouldn't we? How many people do you know who behave like that in your family or among your friends, acquaintances and col-leagues? Isn't it disturbing how small that number is?

If you think that giving to yourself is easy, you might just have jumped the gun. Yes, it may be easier to buy stuff for ourselves than for others, but if that made us happy, why are most of us so miserable? If a girl buys the dress she feels she really must have, and that will make her happy, why is she complaining that there's no space in her wardrobe? Didn't she feel the same about all the other dresses in her wardrobe at some point? Even after buying the new car you've been dreaming of, you find yourself complaining that you have to walk from a secure car park to your house because you don't want to leave it on the street? And you can probably guess what will happen next year when the new model of this car appears.

You've probably heard the phrase: 'Happiness lies within you.' If we really wanted to be happy, we *would* be happy – but for some strange reason people are looking for happiness in the external world rather than within themselves. One Buddhist teacher gave a very good example to demonstrate the absurdity of this situation. Putting a teaspoon of sugar into your drink will make it sweet. The more sugar you add, the sweeter it gets. The same rule should also apply to our happiness as well – the more we have of the thing we like, the happier we should become! Some people say that chocolate cake makes them happy. Eating endless pieces of chocolate cake every day should make them really happy, shouldn't it? They'd probably lose their taste for chocolate cake for quite some time. The same thing could happen even with our parents or friends – we might say that spending time with them makes us happy, but if we spent every minute with them even just for a week, we'd probably want to make a run for it! The same principle applies even with money. Anyone who thinks that money will make them happy, and that the more money they have, the happier they'll become, could be in for a shock. No doubt it has worked for a few people but for most of us more money usually means we want things we didn't consider having before – this only leads to frustration and dissatisfaction as well as a constant desire for something bigger and better, and more and more. People in this trap never really reach the happy state they'd imagined that more money would bring. Yes, we might enjoy the prestigious new car we couldn't afford before, but very soon we'll want a better one. *Spoiler alert* – there's always something bigger and better to wish for – if not now then there will be soon. We don't have to change our lifestyle and become hermits living without any pleasures at all. There's absolutely nothing wrong with wishing for and buying things we like, but we should stop associating our happiness with it. Otherwise, we'll never be happy; and we'll spend our lives chasing rainbows. Seeking freedom from attachments instead will help us take control of our own happiness. Learning to control our desires and state of mind will bring us much more happiness and contentment.

At the same time, education plays a significant role in our lives. And the official education from school or university is probably not the most important form of it. Instead, we learn a lot from life – from our parents, friends, and colleagues as well as from books and so on. We learn how to behave, and how to react to different situations. Learning another language can also give us a fresh perspective on the world as well as on many other things.

You've probably heard the Albert Einstein quote: 'The more I learn, the more I realise how much I don't know.' We're learning all our lives. By improving our skills and knowledge every day we can become a better and more interesting person than we were the previous day – and that's a great thing!

Another important thing we can do is to enhance our physical health – this factor is a big contribution to our happiness. The healthier food we eat, the more we exercise and the more valuable rest we take, the better, the more energetic, exuberant and enthusiastic we'll feel. And that will lift us higher and higher, because we'll have the energy and enthusiasm to do the things we want to do. In turn, we'll have great ideas for our future and will become high achievers. The combination and balance of doing all these small things right will create an enormous positive ripple effect in our lives.

Enhancing our lives and giving to ourselves in this manner will require a lot of time and effort, and it's not as simple as it might appear at first. This type of giving can have a major impact not only on our own lives, but also on the lives of others. The more truly educated, healthy and happy we are, the more we can help ourselves and others.

Just to reinforce the idea of giving to yourself, here are some good reasons for doing so:

Selfish reason 1: *Learning to control our minds and be the masters of our own happiness will free us from suffering. Even if something bad happens, we'll know how to handle the problem and remain happy and calm. As the German philosopher Friedrich Nietzsche* said: 'That which does not kill us makes us stronger'. Also, learning to be grateful for what we have will make our life so much easier and happier.

Selfish reason 2: *Educating ourselves gives us more options in life. We'll find solutions to problems much more easily, and we'll also become more interesting companions. As American author and motivational speaker Jim Rohn states: 'You are the average of the five people you spend the most time with.' We all enjoy the company of like-minded people, and so the more educated and fascinating you are, the more chances you'll have of attracting interesting and successful people. This will increase your own chances of success.*

Selfish reason 3: *The benefits of a healthy, good looking body that radiates energy – should go without saying. Healthy eating and regular exercising will make us feel amazing. There's no doubt that it requires effort, but keep in mind that it's difficult only in the beginning. Once it becomes a habit, it'll be much easier, and you'll definitely find it worthwhile. If you want to avoid a heart attack at the age of 40, and need to take medicines for various health issues, choosing a healthy lifestyle is really the only option. Also, you'll find that being fit and healthy means you'll get more out of holidays and trips. As a more active person, you'll be able to do and see much more, visiting sites of interest in the hills, for example, and saving money on big meals and snacks.*

TYPES OF GIFTS

We make a living by what we get. We make a life by what we give.

—Winston Churchill

We live in a materialistic society where the gifts we give to others are often judged by the price tag. Christmas, for example, is becoming more and more commercialised, and people are lured into buying more items that are also more expensive. The true spirit of this event has been lost for a while now, and the main focus is on buying and receiving gifts. In this way, we unfortunately miss the main point about giving – a gift doesn't necessarily have to be a material item. We'll look at the many different types of gifts in the following chapters.

GIFTS AND FAVOURS

The first type of gift is the most obvious one and represents the most common understanding of the gift. We can give someone a material gift that may be very expensive and exclusive or, on the other hand, it could cost very little. Regardless of the price tag; if the gift is something that's very useful and/or desirable to the recipient, it will bring a lot of joy. A gift could be given without the giver having put any thought into it, but it's generally worth choosing the gift carefully. The recipient will better appreciate something that's specially chosen but inexpensive rather than a very expensive gift that's given without a thought. Such a well-chosen gift can also save us a lot of money. Obviously in this case we'd need to know the receiver personally or be intuitive enough to understand their tastes. There's another very simple option in this situation – give a personalised gift. A champagne flute is not a very good gift, but one that's engraved with a personalised message will be far more precious to the receiver – and we don't even need to know the person that well. Giving Christmas gifts to kids in an orphanage through a charity organisation would be a bit different though, even if we didn't know them – most of the kids would be happy with a toy, and so this wouldn't need too much thought. Another example could involve a family we know of who are struggling with money. They have only two beds for three kids, so two have to share a bed. Giving this family a bunk bed would be a very thoughtful gift they'd really appreciate, even if we'd never met the family.

Giving money to others can be done in various ways. We might decide to give money instead of another type of gift because it's easier and saves us from thinking of what to buy, or because we know that the recipient, at that time, needs money more than anything else. We can donate to charity to help someone indirectly or we can give money directly – to support a football team in our kid's school, for example. We can give money to someone directly such as a homeless person on the street, a musician or someone who finds themselves with insufficient funds to pay for their groceries at a supermarket checkout. We can also give money to someone we know is generally in need.

Favours are not material things, per se, but are sometimes an equivalent. Inviting foster kids to a concert for instance, means we're not giving them money directly, but we're giving them something equivalent, having paid for the tickets. In the same vein, we could fund someone to attend a college, or drive a cancer patient to and from a doctor's appointment once or twice a week. The favours can be very different, but they'll all have the same purpose – to give some kind of service or pleasure to people, to help them out or to enhance their lives in some way.

Gifts, money and favours come at our expense so if you don't feel very charitable, you may be reluctant. Let's try to find some selfish reasons for donating:

Selfish reason 1: *Most people love watching movies with superheroes. You'd probably love to have some superpower yourself that would make you better and stronger than anyone else. Well you can become a superhero to someone who needs help by giving them something they really need. You can be their saviour, and they'll be eternally grateful. And who wouldn't want to be a superhero?*

Selfish reason 2: *This one can help you to keep yourself in shape and feel good. If, for instance, you were planning to buy a cheeseburger or a bar of chocolate for a snack, maybe you could give that snack or £1 to a homeless person and – that way you'll get not two, but three birds with one stone. If you make this a regular habit, you'll stay fit and healthy; you'll make somebody's day; and you'll also feel great by helping that person.*

Selfish reason 3: *By doing favours today, you could be helping yourself in the future. If you help someone now without really expecting to get anything back, you'll find someone who'll be happy to help if you ever need assistance in the future. It's always good to spread kindness.*

Selfish reason 4: Giving money to charities can improve our own life. Donating to a charity for a homeless shelter, for example; will mean there'll be less people on the street asking for money. Alternatively, donating to a charity that plants more trees will mean that you'll be breathing cleaner air in the near future.

TIME

'Time is money', as they say; so by giving our time for someone or something we could say we're, technically, giving money. Time is always precious because there's only a limited amount of it in a day and we can never get it refunded. Few people appreciate the time given to them and so many waste it every day on unimportant things like watching TV or in being angry with someone. Later, unfortunately, many people regret having wasted their time, but they can't turn back the clock. There are so many movies about time travel and different implications for using it incorrectly. One small change today might steer you into a completely different direction in the future. It's like the small angle between two intersecting lines, where the distance between the two lines is very slight at first, but widens as the lines extend.

It's strange how people choose to waste their time in spite of knowing how limited it really is. It's almost as foolish as putting our hand into a pot of boiling water, knowing that it will scald us. Of course, we all need to rest sometimes as no one can be busy all the time without a break. Quality breaks refresh and energise us, helping us to work better. Having a 15-minute power nap, or meditating instead, will make us feel a hundred times more rested than watching TV for the same period. And you know what it's like with TV – once you start watching, you get sucked in, and three or four hours can easily go by in a flash. If you had a headache before, you'll have a bigger one now; your eyes will be tired and your body will be aching from the awkward position you were sitting in while watching TV. So much for resting! On top of that, you'll also be left with the regret that you haven't done anything more productive.

You've probably noticed that some people manage to do a lot more in a day than others do, who just go to work, eat and sleep; and say they have no time for anything else. It's interesting because both types of people have exactly the same number of hours in a day. It all comes down to time management and good planning. Time is one of the most valuable commodities we have in life, and we should therefore appreciate it more. We should relish the quality time that restores us, brings us joy and lifts us up. Instead of watching TV, we could chose to spend time with our partner, kids, family or friends and strengthen our relationships with them. We could go for a longer walk than usual with the dog and play with it in the park, making our pet happy as well as ourselves; we could go to visit our parents or grandparents and share some pleasant memories with them; we could offer help to a friend by listening to their problem and maybe even help to find a solution or we could volunteer at a charity and meet some new people.

In other words, we could put to good use the time we're wasting now. We could use it more constructively and for a good purpose. If we know that 'time is money', then it's just like wasting money. No one benefits: neither us, nor anyone else.

Giving your time to someone can be as difficult as giving your money. Why should you? As usual, the more difficult the task, the more rewarding it will be. Here are just a few examples of how you can benefit by giving your time to others.

Selfish reason 1: You never know when and where the next great thing will happen to you. Volunteering can bring you new friends, great times and laughter, a job offer or even a life or business partner. When such like-minded people gather to help someone, these kind-hearted and generous people communicate and socialise together, and a lot of good things can come out of it.

Selfish reason 2: *Listening to your friend's problems and offering them a shoulder to cry on will teach you a thing or two about life, and you'll understand more about different situations you haven't been in yourself. It's better to learn from other people's mistakes and save yourself from heartache and terrible consequences. Besides, listening to someone telling you about their problems will make you realise how good your own life is in comparison, and you'll be more grateful for what you have.*

Selfish reason 3: *Volunteering for a charity that builds houses will help you to keep fit, you'll spend time in the open air and also learn new skills you could use in the future – you might decide to build your own house one day or just fix something in your existing home.*

Selfish reason 4: *Spending quality time with your family will help you to strengthen the bonds with your partner and children, and create more harmonious relationships. If you have good relationships with your kids, they're more likely to take good care of you when you're old.*

***Selfish reason 5:** As volunteering usually involves meeting and interacting with strangers in one form or another, it'll improve your communication skills as well as boost your self-esteem; especially if you're shy. You'll find these skills really useful in your next job interview or on your next date.*

***Selfish reason 6:** Instead of sitting in front of the TV, spending a few hours among kind and compassionate people to help others will enhance your mood, and give you a sense of purpose.*

KNOWLEDGE AND ADVICE

These days in the Information Age, information has become a very valuable commodity. Having access to data can sometimes be more powerful than having a gun or even an army. Information can be priceless in some cases such as helping someone to win a presidential election, for example. The people in power control the information. Unfortunately, this powerful tool, as any other, is often misused when it's in the wrong hands. Information itself is neither good nor bad – it's just a set of facts. The way the information is used though can give it either positive or negative power. It's the same as water – in its pure form it is our life source, but flooding or hurricanes can be highly destructive.

Information that's distorted and taken out of context can be used to manipulate people and have a very negative result. We frequently see this on the news when it happens in politics, in business and in various other areas of life. The correct information presented in an incorrect form can make people think in a certain way and believe in this, 'the truth', which the ones in power want them to believe. Such manipulation can even change the course of a whole nation when this type of information is used in specific campaigns.

In a perfect world, information would be used constructively to analyse facts and solve problems. After familiarising ourselves with an issue, having the right information can help us find the best solution and take the most appropriate action. At the same time, sharing accurate information with others will help to involve everyone in the positive actions we all need to take to improve our future. Unfortunately, money, greed and profits currently dictate how information is used, but it's just a matter of time before a big change takes place as more and more people have access to accurate information and are helping to spread it even further. When enough people join forces and share their knowledge, they'll support accurate, scientifically proven information and take the initiative towards positive change to steer the world towards a better future. We should all be giving, sharing and spreading positive and correct information – when the motives are good and the power is united, we'll be unstoppable!

Even on a less grand scale, sharing useful information can still help a lot of people. We can share our knowledge with someone, give someone our advice or just spread positive thoughts and insights – these might inspire someone for the greater good. Even a simple thing, like telling a stranger about some discount you think might interest them, or about something positive you just experienced can be very helpful to others. Imagine that while on holiday somewhere, for example; you'd seen an artefact in a castle that amazed you that would have been very easy to miss. When you later overheard someone saying they were about to visit that castle, they'd probably be really glad when you told them about it. It wouldn't cost you anything to tell them but it would help those people to experience something amazing. They could also save some money if you let them know about a special discount that was also available. No doubt you'd like someone to give you tips about interesting and beautiful things to see or places to eat that are not listed in the usual tourist guide; so why not let others benefit from the great things you've discovered?

In another example, let's say you're in a shop and you see a person who can't decide between two similar items. As you've tried both products before, and found one better than the other, why not tell the other person and save them from making the wrong choice?

It's true that sometimes it can be tricky to judge whether or not to intervene in a situation, but a little common sense should help us distinguish between a situation where we can help and one we should stay out of. If we see a mother with a spoiled child acting up in a shop, for example; we probably shouldn't start lecturing her on how she should bring up her child. On the other hand, if we see a mother who is considering buying a toy for her child and we know from experience that the toy will break within a week, maybe we should mention it.

Even though getting information and advice can often cost money; there are always exceptional cases. If, for example; you're a psychotherapist on your way home and you see someone ready to jump off a bridge, it would be inhumane just to walk away without using your knowledge and skills to try and save the person's life unless they're going to pay you the standard hourly rate. Although this is an extreme example, it's sometimes nice to be able to help someone in need. Let's say you're a lawyer and you overhear someone whose rights have been violated in a shop, but they don't realise this due to a lack of knowledge. A sign next to the checkout states that customers cannot return undamaged products. By law, however (at least in some countries), customers *can* return items without any explanation – maybe they just changed their mind. If you see a seller refusing to accept a product for refund, wouldn't you step in and advise the person even though you're usually paid for your advice?

As most of us need to earn a living, we can't give our advice or services freely to everyone, of course. In certain circumstances though, we should be open to helping others. If we don't want to do it for their sake, we should at least do it for our own.

Selfish reason 1: *Sharing information and knowledge can enable people to create effective solutions for all kinds of problems. Once people are well-informed, they can therefore take action to make the world a better place. Don't you want to live in a better world?*

Selfish reason 2: *Helping a stranger will make you feel smarter, superior and also better appreciated – it'll definitely make you feel good.*

Selfish reason 3: If more people help strangers by passing on information or giving advice, it means that, statistically, there's a bigger chance that you'll receive such help when you need it.

FREE THINGS

We all love freebies – whether it's a complementary chocolate served with a coffee, some soap in a hotel room or food samples in a shop. These are all material things and we've already talked about giving material things. Let's talk now about non-material freebies like a genuine smile, a big hug, a compliment, having a laugh or conversation with someone, offering a shoulder to cry on or simply just our presence. We can give these things freely and at the same time, they're priceless. The best thing about these freebies is that there's no limit on how much we can give as there's no danger of breaking the bank.

We can smile at hundreds of people we meet or pass by every day and it'll take nothing from us – on the contrary, we'll actually feel richer and happier at the end of the day. We might have a sore jaw if we take it too far, but that's not the point. Everything is good in moderation. No one is asking you to have the widest smile possible and walk around with it all day long. Even a little smile will still do the trick – lightening up the day for those we smile at as well as for ourselves. Besides, smiles are highly contagious. If you didn't know (it may not be scientifically proven but it's still a fact), try it yourself – when you smile at people they'll nearly always smile back. It's amazing how such a small simple action can have such a powerful effect; changing the mood of everyone and completely changing the atmosphere if you're in an enclosed space as well. And the most awesome thing about it is that it's absolutely free and we can be as generous with it as our jaws allow.

Hugs are another brilliant freebie we can give to others. Maybe this one will have more restrictions on how many, where, when and to whom we should give them; but then again, we're wise people that should be able to recognise the situations appropriate for this wonderful freebie. It's fine to smile at everyone in the shop, but if we start hugging them all, someone might call the security. It's quite different when we meet someone we know though. A greeting and a hug should be the norm. If we see that someone is sad, distressed or even lost, whether we hug them will depend on the acuteness of the situation and whether we know the person or not. If we don't know them, and they're not completely in a panic, we could give them a gentle stroke on the back to express our empathy and support, but without intruding on their personal space too much. Again, such a gesture is free, and it can have a very positive impact on the other person as well as on ourselves. It's worth doing these things as often as appropriate.

This next free thing we can give to other people is so powerful that it's surprising it isn't used more often. A *compliment* can really make someone's day: it can change the course of any conversation; help clinch a business deal or help to avoid an argument. It can also influence positive outcomes in many other situations. A YouTube video shows an interesting social experiment using a mirror. A guy tells girls on the streets and in the park how beautiful the girls behind them are, and when the girls turn around to look, they see his friend holding a mirror. The girls see their own reflections. Not one of them was left without a smile, without laughing or without a warm feeling in their hearts. One of the girls hit an emotional jackpot – from this one very original compliment she got a smile, laughter, a hug, a warm feeling and some tears of joy. It definitely made her day. It's incredible how powerful a compliment can be, but it's often underused or used incorrectly. Some people throw around compliments indiscriminately without any genuine feeling because they want to influence people to favour them in some way. Fake compliments can never have a powerful impression on anyone, and may even have the opposite effect to the one intended. The person will smile and thank you, but will feel there's a hidden agenda behind the compliment. Only the genuine compliments have a positive effect.

The abbreviation 'LOL' is used a lot these days in social media posts and texts, but these three letters fail to unleash the positive power of real-life Laughing Out Loud. Laughter is a magical thing that brings joy to absolutely everyone. No one can really laugh genuinely and feel unhappy in the same moment. Maybe the problems won't just disappear and the person will still need to deal with them after having a good laugh, but at the moment of laughter people allow themselves to be free from problems. In that magical moment, we feel happy, hopeful, optimistic and free from worries. Laughter can have very powerful healing qualities that benefit our psychological and physical health. We could give so much joy to people whether we know them or not just by having lots of laughs with them and spreading the good mood.

To give joy to people we don't necessarily have to be comedians and make them laugh like mad. Even a simple conversation with a stranger, acquaintance or, of course, with someone we love can be a very joyful experience to both parties, especially to anyone who feels lonely or left out. Now, there are services where volunteers hold conversations with elderly people, and this reflects the serious problem of seniors feeling left out, forgotten and lonely. There's actually a high demand for these conversation partners. Everyone needs to feel part of a group and belong to a social circle; they need to feel they're part of the community. Being part of something bigger than ourselves gives us a place and a sense of purpose. Many people avoid interacting with others for various reasons, but only a handful of people are genuinely and truly happy being completely alone without any communication or conversation with others. Most of us have days when we really want to be alone and would give anything for a couple of hours just to be left in peace, but such retreats from others are brief, and most of the time we long for company and conversation.

Sometimes there's a need for more than just a simple conversation when people have problems and they're desperate for a shoulder to cry on. At moments like this, people not only need to talk to dispel their loneliness, but they also need the support and compassion of the listener. When we have a problem, we tend to exaggerate the intensity of the issue and believe we're the only one with a problem like that. We feel the need for a shoulder to cry on. We wouldn't hesitate to offer such help to someone we love, but might be more reluctant to give it to a stranger. We should be more kind and compassionate though; even with people we don't know. That's because we're all connected and we're all human beings; and suffering is suffering regardless of our relationship to a particular person.

It's much easier to feel the pain of the ones we love because we know them. We understand the situation they're in, and feel strong compassion towards them. But we can still give to people who we've never met before, simply by offering our presence. Just letting them know they're not alone, without any other actions, will make them feel safer and more at ease. We don't necessarily have to offer our shoulder to cry on or hold lengthy conversations to discuss all their problems – in some situations, our presence is all that's needed. For example, if you saw a lost and distressed child in the shopping centre, you wouldn't just ask a staff member to announce the information about the lost kid, and then walk away. You'd probably stay with the child until the parents come to the meeting point announced, to make sure the kid is ok and feels safe. Or, if your own kids are scared of the dark, you'd stay with them next to the bed until they fell asleep.

Likewise, simply our presence can make another person feel safe. It might seem like something small to us, but it could mean a great deal to them.

There are so many free gifts we can give to other people, and there's no reason why we shouldn't do that. Another important thing to understand is that our free gift might mean the world to the receiver at that moment even though it cost us nothing and we really thought nothing of it. If, for whatever reason, you still don't want to give your time or company or any other freebie for the benefit of others, you might want to start giving these thing for your own benefit instead.

Selfish reason 1: It's scientifically proven that smiling enhances mood and has a positive effect on our health. If you don't want to smile at strangers to make them happy, then do it for your own benefit and well-being.

Selfish reason 2: If you give someone a hug in their moment of need, and give genuine compliments to people every day, you'll soon become very popular and likeable wherever you go. And who doesn't want to be popular? It might even lead to a promotion at work or some other great benefit.

Selfish reason 3: The healing power of laughter is even greater than that of a smile, and we all want to be healthy. Also by laughing a lot and making other people laugh, you'll be popular with everyone.

Selfish reason 4: *Practice makes perfect. The more you practise your communication skills, the better they'll be. Before long, you'll see that no situation can catch you off guard. Tasks like job interviews will be a piece of cake.*

Selfish reason 5: *Volunteering might actually give you an interesting hobby as well as a good time. You could add new meaning to your life, make new friend or even meet someone who becomes your partner. You could also find a great job opportunity.*

GIVING ALONG THE WAY WITHOUT ANY EFFORT OR EXPENSE

Generally speaking, people understand giving something to someone as involving money or some other material gift. It can also mean giving time or performing a service of one sort or another. The giver decides to give something for the benefit of the person in need. Sometimes, people are a bit reluctant to give because they're not ready or happy to do so – they think they also need that money or that they never have time for themselves, let alone for others.

Therefore, it's great news for people like that because we can find ways to give to others and be kind and compassionate without spending a single penny, and without wasting any of our precious time. Imagine, for example; that you're on your way to work, and in front of you is a man pushing an old lady in a wheelchair. When the front wheel gets stuck in a hole, the man struggles to free the wheelchair, and all you need to do is lean over a little and lift the front of the wheelchair slightly to release the wheel. Even if you're in a hurry, you can easily help as you're passing. It'll cost you nothing, and will only take a second.

Imagine you need to pick up a couple of things in the city centre and you've parked in a place where you paid the minimum charge, which is for one hour. When you return to the car after only 20 minutes, you see another driver approaching the parking machine to pay for parking. You could stop them and ask if they're planning to stay for less than 40 minutes, and offer them your ticket if they are. This small act of giving will cost you nothing, and you won't have another chance to use the ticket in any case. Some people might say: 'Yes, but I paid for my ticket so why should I give it to somebody else? In this case you could look at the situation in reverse – if you came to the city centre to quickly do a few things, and needed only 30 minutes or so but found you had to pay for the minimum parking time of an hour, you'd probably be thrilled when someone stepped in and offered you a free ticket for 40 minutes!

In another example, imagine you were enjoying a city break with a friend; walking around some beautiful streets and admiring the architecture. You went into a small pizzeria and ordered two pizzas. You both find the pizzas very tasty and filling, and there are two slices left. You could either force yourselves to finish them and end up feeling bloated and lazy, deciding not to resume your stroll, or you could leave the leftover slices on the plate for the staff to throw away. Alternatively, you could place the slices on a napkin and hand it to a disabled beggar outside. Maybe giving away leftovers like this wouldn't work well with messier kinds of food that needs to be eaten using cutlery, but this works perfectly well with pizza – it's easy to handle, and each slice is separate, and hasn't been touched in the process of eating. Here again is a good deed that really costs nothing in terms of time or money.

All it requires is a little kindness and compassion. Seeing the situation from another person's perspective makes us a better, more thoughtful person. There's nothing to stop you from doing this kind of good deed, but if you still have any doubts, let's look at some selfish reasons for doing so.

Selfish reason 1: *Being a good and helpful person feels pretty amazing. You can be a great help to someone with very little effort, and even without spending anything.*

Selfish reason 2: *You can feel proud of yourself when you help someone. How else can you feel this satisfaction for doing something that involves so little effort? Usually you need to put a lot of time and effort into achieving something before you can have this sense of pride.*

Selfish reason 3: *Even if you have enough money, it's still very satisfying to get free city centre parking. And if this practice of ticket-sharing spread, you'd soon be on the receiving end of it too!*

GIFT GIVEN ≠ GIFT RECEIVED

I know what I have given you...
I do not know what you have received.

—Antonio Porchia

Often in business, marketing a product focuses more on the benefit the consumer will receive than on the product itself. The product could actually be something very simple and cheap to produce, but very often what we pay for is the feeling of satisfaction we get from the added value and benefit. If we analyse the actual product to see what it's made of; its structure, form and shape as well as the cost of producing it; we'll get a different picture from the one in the ad. A mobile phone, for example, is just a small, slim rectangular gadget with a touch screen. Any smart-phone will have similar features, but certain phones will make you cool and more popular – and this has more to do with the image of the product than with the actual product itself. At the same time, and regardless of the type of phone it is, the device gives us the opportunity to communicate with others, no matter how far away they are. The internet service and the many apps for phones also allow you to follow the news, do some work and even give you travel directions. We therefore value the phone not for what it is but rather, for what it allows us to do. The same principle applies when giving to others. Our gift, whether it's time, a donation or a hug is the small thing we give, similar to the phone that is simply a product; but the actual gift that someone receives is more about the benefits, just as with the phone. The gift received might far outweigh the value of the actual thing that's given, bringing the extra benefits of pleasant emotions, satisfaction and even happiness.

GIFTS

We'll see every little thing we give transforming like a caterpillar into a butterfly, and bringing a smile to the faces of others. The money we donate to charity can be used to satisfy basic everyday needs such as food, warm clothes or shoes. It can be spent on the treatment, or even the cure for a disease. It can fund people needing to rebuild their home after a natural disaster or used to improve the quality of life for a family by providing basic items like a bed for every child in the family – things that most of us just take for granted. The effective use of donations, in fact; can secure a better and happier future where we'll not be scared to lose our loved ones to a terminal disease with no available treatment. Our donations can help save the environment and provide us with more trees and cleaner air to bring a sustainable future, and hopefully fewer wars over energy resources. After all, no one can have a monopoly over the sun and wind (except in the children's story Chipollino and the 'World's most outrageous taxes' where the government puts taxes on the air and rain; but that's very unlikely to happen in the real world).

The money we give or donate can be converted into all kinds of different things that people need from the smallest thing like a sandwich to a very big the thing like saving somebody's life. If we all come together for one cause, we can achieve great things. Giving as little as £1 can change someone's life and brighten up the future for everybody. If everyone does the same, it can change the world.

If you sometimes think that we're not powerful enough to change the world, you're quite wrong. You should know that you can at least change someone's life. Any gift we give to someone in need means much more to them than it does to us. We tend to take too many things for granted and might not understand the value of small everyday things. If we give a dining table and chairs to a poor family, we'll be giving them more than just a table. We'll be giving them the opportunity to enjoy a nice family time, all sitting together for their meals. We'll also be giving their kids a more appropriate place for doing their homework as well as for any drawing or colouring they'd like to do; allowing them to sit straight and have good posture with less chance of back problems in the future. Alternatively, we might give them the use of an office space if any of the adults work from home sometimes and have office facilities. And we give them dignity, joy and something they'd wanted for ages, but couldn't have.

Helping an animal that's vulnerable and can't help itself can be transformative. An injured animal can't do much to help itself, and may, therefore, depend on the kindness of rescuers. Saving an animal is not limited to giving them a good bath, medicine, food and shelter – we can give them a new life and family in a safe place as well as food, love and joy. If we look at pictures or videos of pets before and after rescue, we can see the huge difference that good care can make. The sad, scared and possibly abused animal with lowered head and ears down in the 'before' picture is almost unrecognisable when compared to the one in the 'after' picture. The creature no longer crouches but its head is lifted up, its ears are facing upwards and it appears a healthy, lively animal that is full of joy. Dogs especially will feel grateful for the rest of their lives, and would probably give their life for the person who saved them and took care of them. My aunt took home a dog that had been hit by a bus and that may have been mistreated by its previous owner. Several bones were broken; he was in pain and was naturally behaving in a very aggressive manner. My aunt covered him with a warm jacket, took him to a vet for treatment, then fed him and gave him a soft cushion, leaving him to sleep on the landing outside her apartment at first–she lived on the top floor and was the only one who used that landing. Soon the dog realised that she was a friend and not a foe, and stopped trying to bite her. She then took him to live with her in her apartment, surrounding him with lots of love and care. He was about one-and-a-half years old when she found him, and lived for around seventeen years, which is fairly old for a dog. The dog was devoted to her and would even allow her to take the bone he was chewing out of his mouth. He would raise his lip to express dissatisfaction, but would never even growl at her, let alone bite.

Vulnerable children also deserve our help. Donating gifts to an orphanage or contributing to the cost of medical treatment for kids that are ill is very worth-while, and again, gifts that are small to us will mean a lot to them. If we can befriend the children, and let them feel our love and care, they'll feel more secure and less alone, they can feel hope and happiness, and they can dream. By looking at the bigger picture, we can understand that kids are vulnerable and depen-dent on our kindness, regardless of whether they're in an orphanage, are sick or live happy and healthy lives. Also, the gifts and everything else we give to our own kids could have a huge impact on their future. Sometimes though, it's best to refrain from giving too many things to our kids. Limiting the amount of sweets and junk food will help them to have a healthy body, and to develop healthy habits. Pushing them to learn another language, to play the piano or learn any other skill, is a gift and investment for their future they'll be grateful for and will appreciate much later. Our kids might get their dream job or meet their life partner because of something we gave them when they were growing up.

So again, the things that are received can be differ-ent from what is given. The gifts can change in form, such as the money spent on things that are needed, so that a gift that had only a small value to us can be of huge value to the recipient. A gift given with added care and love might even save someone's life and bring happiness. And the benefits from a gift, such as music tuition, will be received many years later. So let's be compassionate, kind and thoughtful when we give because the benefits from the right gift can grow and change in positive ways. Unfortunately, the reverse is also true as a very small, but negative action can also grow and change into something much bigger and much worse than we could have imagined. We need to be aware of the effects of our actions and of what we create and spread in the world – let our actions be positive ones with positive effects.

EMOTIONS

Pleasant emotions are the hidden and unexpected bonuses that come from giving, and that both the giver and receiver can enjoy. The various emotions they're likely to experience may include pride, serenity and inspiration as well as joy, hope, love and gratitude. The strength and intensity of these feelings will differ from one situation to another and will have all different kinds of positive impact both on the giver and receiver.

Most givers feel pride at the moment of giving. Even though their act of kindness may have been small, they feel they did the right thing, and the good deed makes them feel they're a good person. This great feeling can continue for hours, and maybe for the rest of the day. It's a very positive emotion because it not only makes us feel good at the time, but also inspires us to perform further good deeds in the future, and spread kindness all around. On one occasion I put together a few food bags with a sandwich, a muffin, an apple and a bottle of water in each, and went into the city centre to give the bags to homeless people. At first I was disappointed because I didn't see any homeless people, and felt a bit stupid walking around with food bags and no one to give them to. It's not that I wished there were more homeless people; it would be best if there were none, of course. But knowing that they were there, and I couldn't find them was frustrating. When I eventually found a beggar and gave him a food bag, it was a very joyful moment. Quite a few passers-by gave me huge smiles, and one guy even gave me a thumbs-up. The thought that I might have inspired at least one of these people to do something good on that day or in the future made me really happy. One simple and very small act of kindness generated so many positive emotions: pride, inspiration, joy and happiness. Such actions also give us serenity and peace within ourselves because we know we've done the right thing, and have nothing to regret. Later, when we look back at what we've achieved, there's nothing but positivity and a good feeling in our hearts.

The receivers experience slightly different emotions from the givers. Getting a gift, no matter how small, can have a very big meaning if it's something we really need – it gives us joy and satisfaction. At the same time, all kinds of positive emotions come along with the gift. Gratitude is probably the strongest one. If someone steps in to help us when we're not expecting anything, we naturally feel very grateful. It also gives us hope that there's a light at the end of the tunnel, and that the bad times we're going through now can, with the help of others, turn into something good. Knowing that there are good people out there who are ready to offer a helping hand gives us hope for humanity and hope for a better future. The love that we feel when someone shows us kindness is very precious – it gives us a warm feeling in our heart and stops us from feeling lost and lonely at that moment. As a receiver, we not only get the gift, but we also get the uplifting positive emotions. The best proof of the overwhelming amount of the emotions flooding through us is our tears of joy.

It's an interesting paradox that the person who gives actually gets more than the one who receives.

You'd think that the giver would be losing or sacrificing something in order to benefit another, but that simply isn't true. The positive emotions the giver experiences are at least three times greater than those the receiver feels. Think about it. The other person receives the gift and feels positive emotions. They feel happy now they've got the thing they needed. The giver, on the other hand, feels happy for at least three reasons: they're pleased to make the other person happy; they're happy for themselves because it feels great to help others; and they feel happy for the others who were inspired by seeing the act of kindness. And that's just the start of it. They can also be glad that the compassion and kindness will most likely be spread – those who received help are more likely to help others in the future; and those who enjoyed seeing someone helping are also more likely to give their kindness and help someone as well – hopefully creating a knock-on effect. And with a small act of kindness, the giver will feel happy to be spreading the wave of positivity and contributing to a better world as the value of the original gift grows and grows.

SHARING IS CONTAGIOUS

Love only grows by sharing. You can only have more for yourself by giving it away to others.

—Brian Tracy

We've all come across videos or stories that went viral online when people kept sharing them. There are also plenty of good stories and amazing videos that don't go viral, mainly due to a smaller number of shares and likes. In many cases, the viral videos are not necessarily the best ones, but they have the numbers. In the ones that go viral though, there is something that triggers one of the strong emotions, such as amusement, compassion, love or awe, which makes people want to like and share that story. Sometimes we also see negative videos, photos or stories that people share because they want to raise awareness of an issue and stop the negativity from spreading by uniting people against it. Regardless of whether the posts being shared are negative or positive, the shares are driven by the emotions the video, photo or story evoke. By encouraging positive emotions, we can raise awareness of the things we can achieve when we unite our goals, so that sharing and giving will become second nature to us.

CONTINUITY WITHIN THE GROUP

In former times, our sense of community was much stronger, and people felt the need to belong to some kind of community. These days, people tend to be a bit disconnected as everyone fights for their own survival. We do still have a lingering sense of community though, and that gets stronger when we form some kind of group.

A group of close friends usually share things freely among themselves. Girls like to borrow a dress or a bag when they're planning to go to a party or on a date. Another time, a different member of that group might borrow shoes or a bracelet, and so on. It all started with one person giving something to another, and it continued in the same manner, soon becoming quite natural for them to share things. The same works in families. When a woman gives her love to her husband, it makes him feel happy and appreciated, and so he naturally wants to return the same love and care, if not more, to his wife. When there are loving parents, the kids are happy. They love their parents in return, and tend to behave well. The kids pass on their love to their pets and the pets bring a lot of joy to the family that loves them, and so on and so forth.

Giving and sharing is contagious and it circulates within the group. It is eternal energy that flows and spreads the positivity in our hearts. But unfortunately, the opposite is also true when someone sends out negative energy. One person's bad behaviour will have little effect if we react with love and care, but most people react differently. Most of us are likely to feel agitated and express anger. We might even develop hatred towards the offending person. By responding with negativity, however, we only create more of the same, and worsen the situation. It's therefore important to understand that we can't fight hatred with hatred – it will cause a lot of unnecessary pain as well as dissatisfaction all round. We can only fight hatred with love; and love, like giving, is very contagious.

You might say that the example of a loving family where love flows from one person to another and everyone feels happy, is rare, and that half the husbands and wives actually hate and resent each other instead. That may be true, and the reason for it is not a lack of love, but rather a lack of knowledge of how to show it, and a lack of compassion and empathy towards the other person. There's often an inability to see things from the other person's perspective. Gary Chapman, in his helpful and enlightening book, *The Five Love Languages*, explains how to recognise these languages and how to improve our relationships. He looks at the relationships between parents and kids, and between colleagues or friends as well as the romantic ones. The book is well worth reading – personally, I'd like to see it taught in schools, as it would help all kinds of relationships to be more successful, leaving us all much happier as well as preventing many divorces in the future. The principle is simple: we usually express our love in the way we want to get it ourselves, but that's not necessarily the way the other person wants to receive it – and that's just how dissatisfaction and resentment arise. When I mentioned the book to a friend, he instantly thought of one couple he knew who probably wouldn't have got divorced if they'd read it. The author also supports the idea that hatred and resentment will disappear when approached with love. We can't expect people to react to love straight away though; it needs time to sink in where the other person has bad feelings in their heart from the past. Quite a few movies are based on this idea, demonstrating how love and care can win over even the most angry and rebellious hearts. In the movie *Coach Carter*, a basketball coach helps a group of teenagers to become a winning team and also to excel in class. This was a tough form of love that met with a lot of resistance from the kids; but with care, determination and out of a genuine wish to help, the coach eventually won them over. These kinds of changes don't happen overnight though. We need to be both consistent and persistent with our love and kindness and not allow any negative feelings to develop that will make us respond with anger.

You've probably worked somewhere where you hated some of the people. You may have found them very difficult, and wished they'd leave; or maybe you yourself wanted to find another job. But if you try to remember how the problem between you started, you'll probably find it was your reaction to something bad, or more correctly perhaps, something the person had done that you perceived as bad. Instead of giving them love and trying to understand their perspective, you reacted with anger, and it's been like a game of ping pong between you both ever since.

Even though some people have behaved badly towards us, we should try to understand them before judging them and labelling them as 'bad people'. They may have had an argument with their spouse, and then projected their anger onto us because they needed to release the negative energy. But luckily, just as love and compassion can be disrupted by bad behaviour and negative emotions, the chain of bad feelings and behaviour can be interrupted and broken with kindness. So if we understand how giving and sharing are contagious, why don't we spread love and joy to bring happiness into the groups and communities we really care about?

PAY IT FORWARD

Sometimes, showing compassion within our own group is difficult, let alone giving our kindness to strangers. The amazing movie *Pay it Forward* brought me to tears. When a little boy came up with a great idea for his school project, the idea really caught on. His idea was: 'When someone does you a big favour, don't pay it back... pay it forward!' When one person does something good for three people and these three people each do something good for another three, we have a geometric progression in which the number of people receiving help expands exponentially.

The YouTube video 'Life Vest Inside – Kindness Boomerang – One Day' illustrates a similar idea, although in this case, one person helps only one other person instead of three. Obviously it's an invention, but it is based on real life. Although not many positive actions will spread or come back to us as quickly as in that 5-minute video, the principle is the same. Kindness, care and love spread very easily and we should never tire of spreading these things.

It's wonderful if we can spread good and positive things and feelings throughout our lives. Maybe we think it's impossible and too idealistic, but we really can achieve it with some effort. It's not actually very hard. All we need to do is show our kindness to three people, and if we could do that every day, we'd help to make everyone in the world feel happy. It's very simple maths, I know a lot of people don't like maths, but now there are different tools online that can help us to calculate figures quite easily. I tried it out and calculated the geometric progression for this situation: if we start from one person helping three others; then they help another three people, and so on. We have our first term of sequence as 1 and the common ratio as 3, and we know that there are 7.5 billion people in the world. The first term is 1, the second is 3 (1*3), the third is 9 (3*3), so after just two steps, 12 people received help (3+9). To reach everyone, we need as little as 22 terms because the number of all people who received help will grow exponentially to 15.6 billion.

It seems difficult to believe that by starting from one person sharing something with as few as three people, we could reach everyone so quickly; but suddenly it seems more feasible. Just imagine what we could achieve if every single one of us made only a small effort. We could all do it together. No task would be too big for us. There would be nothing we couldn't achieve. No problem would be too complex for us to solve. If we all act together, we can achieve anything. And the best thing is that we don't need to move a mountain – we just need to start by moving a small stone, and play our part with small acts of kindness to spread love.

SEEING THINGS FROM A DIFFERENT PERSPECTIVE

A truly compassionate attitude toward others does not change even if they behave negatively or hurt you.

—Dalai Lama

As people are very different, they all perceive things differently. Something that seems good to one person can be negatively perceived by another. There's no absolute truth, everything is relative and everything acquires good or bad qualities depending on the situation, on the context and on our views. For example, laughter is generally considered as something good that brings joy, health and happiness, but if the laughter comes at a funeral or in a serious job interview, it would have a different effect, and would be considered rude and inappropriate. Things look different when we change our perspective or angle, or our environment. Every driver knows about the blind spot at the side of the car – the area that is not visible in any of the mirrors. If you've ever looked at any pictures of optical illusions, you'll know how the shape or form that's depicted can appear as different things at the same time. Lines that are parallel, for example, appear otherwise, or we can see two quite different objects depending on the angle we look at, or just by shaking our head. One summer when I lived in Scotland, my parents came to visit and I took them to Loch Lomond for a boat ride. It was a pleasant sunny day (one of the few in the year in Scotland) and we took lots of great photos. A few weeks later my brother and aunt visited me and I repeated the trip with them. This time it was typical Scottish weather with a grey sky and rain all day. The place we visited was the same, but the conditions had changed and so the scenery was completely different. Both scenes of Loch Lomond have their own beauty, but the pictures from the sunny day bring back the good memories, whereas the ones of the gloomy day remind me of the rain and cold rather than of any good emotions on that day.

Nothing in the world is an absolute truth; everything in life depends on our perception. We can look at literally anything from different perspectives. Even the most evil thing in the world has the potential to become good if we change the circumstances. Perhaps it's not the most pleasant example, but even killing someone, which seems fundamentally a bad thing, can become good in certain circumstances. If we were in a remote place with someone who had no chance of recovering from their serious injuries, where there was little hope of getting any immediate medical help, and doctors would be unable to save the person in any case, the person could stay alive for only a few more minutes. Would it be better to leave them in unbearable pain or help them to die? Another example of something that appears bad but can be used in a positive way is the bomb. These days it has very negative associations, and is linked with terrorist acts, fear and a lot of victims, but such explosive devices can also be used in a positive way in construction work or in building a canal or tunnel, for instance. Again, the thing itself is, in fact, neither good nor bad, but we perceive the way it's used as positive or negative. The time we live in can affect our perception, and the context can also colour our thinking. Something that was considered good or normal two hundred years ago, may be seen in a completely different light today, for example. We used to think the Earth was flat until our perception of it changed. We need to open ourselves to the possibility that the way we view the world is not necessarily the best way. There could be unknown possibilities that could help us change with time and reach our highest self. Even if we don't feel ready to give to others, perhaps we'll really enjoy doing it once we give it a try. Maybe we'll like it so much that we won't be able to imagine how we'd lived before without giving.

EVOLUTION THROUGH OUR LIFETIME

We probably weren't the biggest advocates of sharing in our childhood. If we had brothers and sisters, we probably ended up fighting a lot of the time. It wasn't that we didn't love our siblings though – quite the opposite – we just had that urge to fight for everything we considered as ours. In the biggest room in the house there'd be a space on the floor where we'd want to draw or play, and our siblings would want that space as well so we'd fight with them even though there was plenty of room for us all. That's a typical scenario. In a funny video about sibling love ('Geschwisterliebe') where a brother and sister are fighting over the food, the mother's reaction is brilliant. The video illustrates how siblings will fight just for the sake of fighting. Even though there's plenty of food available, they just don't want to share and can't bear the idea of the sibling getting a slightly bigger portion. Children who have no siblings can have even bigger issues with sharing, simply because they haven't practised it with siblings at home. They may have trouble adapting after joining a kindergarten and suddenly having to share the toys with other kids as they don't really understand the concept of sharing.

We have more experience of sharing as teenagers. If we have siblings, we even start covering up for each other and joining in a pact against our parents. Again, it's not that we don't love them; it's just that we're at the rebellious age when the people with the biggest influence on us are no longer our parents but our peers. Our siblings can be our friends or foes at this stage, depending on the age difference between us. We share most of our time and emotions with the friends around us while being dismissive of our parents' love and wish to connect with us. We even get angry with our parents for trying to control us and for not letting us do everything we want, while accusing them of not caring about us at the same time. We don't consider our parents perspective at all, and feel sure that our way of doing things and our views are the only ones that are true. And it's not only our parents we feel don't understand us when we're teenagers – all the adults seem to conspire against to make our lives miserable. From our perspective at that time it seems that our parents are being controlling by not letting us go to that party or concert, or by stopping us from hitchhiking to the seaside. We don't see the situation from our parent's perspective at all, although they're trying to protect us and maybe even save our lives.

When we reach our mid-twenties, and especially if we have kids of our own, we start seeing things from our parents' perspective. Sometimes we even feel like apologising for our bad behaviour as teenagers, and thank them for trying to take care of us. Our views and values change and we start to see things differently when we become parents ourselves. We start to become more giving and caring now that we have a lot more kindness in our heart, together with a wish to help others. We often disregard our own needs for the sake of others; ready to step in and help whenever needed.

When we get older we become more and more giving and ready to help. Maybe it's due to experience and a little wisdom as well as realising that we can't take our material possessions with us. Also, the joy we experience in giving encourages us to do even more. Grandparents usually have a huge amount of love to give to their grandkids, and enjoy looking after them and reading them stories as well as teaching them and sharing their life experiences with them.

Everyone changes throughout their lifetime. Our bodies are constantly changing; our state of health can fluctuate; and our thought patterns and opinions also often change. In fact, we're not ever really the same for two days in a row. Time moves on, and we move with it. If we accept that we're subject to constant change, why not make the changes positive? We can benefit from studying ourselves and trying to analyse our emotions, and by learning from others. Why wait until you're older? By starting to give now, you can enhance your life from today.

THE PARENTAL PERSPECTIVE MAKES MORE SENSE

Parents, especially mothers, have the primary instinct to protect and care for their children. The maternal instinct is so strong that if you would describe it in a different situation it would sound insane. There's a video on YouTube you might have seen about the 'World's Toughest Job', where people are interviewed for the fake job of 'Director of Operations' that's presented as the most important job in the world. This job entails working for 24 hours a day with a lot of it standing and bending; there are no breaks and you can have lunch only after your associates have had theirs. The job requires good negotiation and interpersonal skills as well as some knowledge of medicine, finance and the culinary arts. There are no vacations, and the workload will actually increase during holidays. Your associates will require a lot of attention and you may even need to stay up all night with them on occasions. If the job is very demanding, the rewards are also very great. The strong relationships you make and the affection you receive from helping them are benefits that are immeasurable. Finally, the job takes up 365 days a year and is an unsalaried position. The interviewees said these conditions were inhuman and crazy, and that no one would want to do this job. They were naturally very surprised when the interviewer told them that billions of people were already doing it. When they asked who these people were, he answered: 'Moms, and they meet every requirement'. The surprise realisation brought everyone to laughter and tears!

The lengths we can go to for our children can sometimes be unbelievable. If our kid misbehaves, we don't think he or she is bad and don't stop talking to them or loving them. But if someone else we know misbehaves, we're very quick to judge and label them as bad – we might even decide to just cut them out of our lives altogether. If our kids, especially as teenagers, shout at us and treat us as their enemies, we still see them as good people who are just going through a rough phase. We still see the potential good in them, and know that the anger is just on the outside. If our friend, colleague or partner shouted at us and treated us as badly as our teenage children do, our reaction would be completely different though. We'd be unlikely to give them the benefit of the doubt or consider them as a nice person who just had an angry episode. We wouldn't see much good in them at that moment and probably wouldn't feel much love towards them. We react to exactly the same situation with a completely different approach then when our child is not involved – in that case, we're understanding, loving, kind and compassionate. With anyone else though, we tend to be angry, unforgiving, judgmental and unsympathetic. Why is the situation so different?

You might say 'oh, but that's my kid'. How is it then that we can show kindness and care towards other kids as well, but not to adults? If some kids in a shop were acting up, for example, and, perhaps throwing some of the goods around, or making a lot of noise in a restaurant and throwing cutlery about, we would see it as a disgrace. We might wonder why the parents hadn't brought them up a bit better; but on the whole, we'd be forgiving and excuse them by saying 'they're just kids'. On the other hand, though; we'd probably feel horrified and resentful seeing an adult acting like that; and we wouldn't want to give them a second chance unless the person was disabled, in which case we might be a bit more forgiving and sympathetic. It seems that an adult has no right to and doesn't deserve any sympathy, kindness or compassion. Why we can't be compassionate towards all living beings regardless of their age or experience? Do we actually think that adults know better and that they have all figured everything out? That just isn't true. People with a lot of experience still make mistakes, even when they're old. Some have never had a good example in their family of how to behave, so they might not fit in with the 'normal' behaviour in society, having quite a different understanding of 'normal' themselves. And who can blame them? We probably can't even blame their parents because their situation may have been similar. How can we fail to have compassion for people who were raised in difficult circumstances? Kids are very susceptible and they inevitably imitate their parent's behaviour and relationships. Of course we all have the power to change our lives and everything depends on us, but not everyone is strong enough to do it. When two brothers, one alcoholic and the other a successful business man, were asked about the reason for their present circumstances, both gave the same answer 'because my dad was an alcoholic'. The same situation can be an excuse for one person, and a lesson for the future for another.

Animals, as well as humans, often tend to differentiate between the young and the adults of their kind, treating young animals differently, and sometimes even showing kindness to a young animal even when the adults of that species are rivals. You might have seen the videos on YouTube of animals adopting young orphaned animals, feeding them and taking care of them. The maternal instinct can actually be stronger than the natural instinct of species. Dogs and cats; cats and mice; tigers and pigs; hunting dogs and rabbits; lions and monkeys – these animals are not naturally the greatest of friends, as one would normally be the predator and the other would be the prey. But when it comes to baby animals and mothers, however, the maternal instinct can suddenly override the natural instinct, and affection and care is given to the young one.

If many animals can sometimes act against their natural instincts to take care of the young of other species, why shouldn't we treat adults in need with an open heart? Many adults feel lost, and are unsure of what they're doing like babies in a way. They often need our help and guidance as they long for someone to take care of them when they have difficulties. At the

least, they need a helping hand or a little encourage-
ment to make them feel they're not alone.

EXTENDING OUR GIFTS TO OTHERS

Please don't worry; no one expects you to suddenly
start loving everyone as much as you love your kids,
or to give away all your possessions to become like
Mother Teresa. That would be like starting a strict
exercise routine with 100 sit-ups, 100 push-ups and 100
squats on the first day. The idea is to start by opening
up our minds to the possibility of being kind-hearted towards others. Just by keeping an open mind,
you can achieve miracles in time. Following the same
example of exercising; by reminding ourselves of the
health benefits and of how we'll look and feel amazing
once we get on with it instead of thinking about how
hard it is; we'll soon feel more positive about it. Even
though we know it's hard, we can set ourselves very
sensible targets in the beginning. To avoid straining
ourselves, we can start from doing each exercise 5
times a day for the first week, increasing to 10 times
a day in the second week and then 15 times a day in
the third week. After six months, 100 sit-ups, 100
push-ups and 100 squats will be easy compared to
how it was in the beginning. If we started by attempt-

ing 100 repetitions of each exercise a day, we'd never do it because it would seem impossible. But if we view that number as a longer term goal, and start with just 5, we'll soon notice how our understanding of what's possible expands every day.

The same principle applies when showing kindness and compassion to others. We just need to open our minds to the possibility that we can start by feeling kindness towards others. All we need to do is to start noticing our thoughts and feelings, and try to understand our reactions to different situations and people. When we encounter a person who behaves in a way we dislike, we can imagine for a moment that this adult is like a kid who might feel lost, angry, scared or insecure. Although adopting this habit might not make us feel any kindness or compassion for that person straight away, we will feel less angry towards them, and start to open our minds to a different way of thinking – it takes time to change our attitudes and habits. After some time, as we become more aware of our attitudes and notice our reactions to situations and people, we'll soon start to understand ourselves better, and may see the potential for goodness in others too. We'll start to separate people from their bad behaviour and understand that they aren't intrinsically bad; only their behaviour is bad – just as we feel about our kids.

We don't say that someone is a cancerous person if they have cancer, but we do say someone is an angry person when they express anger. If we could understand negative emotions as we do a disease, we could easily see that a particular person is good in normal conditions but is temporarily displaying their negative emotions. Throw a stone at me if you've never felt at least a little angry in your life. Even very spiritual people have felt angry at some time because they weren't born in that enlightened state, but followed a path to reach it. If you were angry with someone and maybe even had an argument with them that involved shouting, they'd see you as a terrible angry person. But are you? Do you think of yourself as bad and angry? No? Then why can't you view others in the same way?

Here's another analogy that can help us see the good in people. When the sky is cloudy and we can't see the sun, we don't assume that the sky is always cloudy and there's never any sunshine. We know that the sun is still there and the dark clouds are only a temporary disruption in a pure blue sky on a sunny day. Similarly, we manage to see the potential in our kids even when they behave badly. Every adult also has potential. Adults may have more dark clouds around them than kids do, but they've probably had more negative experiences to produce those dark clouds. Bad experiences and circumstances are not at all an excuse for negative emotions though, and every single person has the potential to feel a lot more positive. It's within our power to dispel the dark clouds and let the sunshine in to warm and uplift our spirit.

The least we can do is open our mind to the possibility that other people are good and have the potential for positive thoughts – this understanding will make us feel they're more worthy of our compassion and kindness. When we start treating everyone with the same kindness that we have in our hearts for our kids, we'll begin to see the change. Maybe at first it'll seem that a 'bad' person will not react positively to our new attitude because they're used to being treated differently, but eventually they'll start to mellow and respond more positively. When we suddenly change and start showing kindness and compassion, we shouldn't expect the other person to respond well immediately, especially if we'd previously reacted to them with the same anger and disrespect as they'd shown us. They probably will respond negatively at first, but we need to give them time. When our kids are acting up, we know it'll only be temporary. We give them one chance after another because we still believe in them and see the good in them.

Most of the time the anger or disappointment we feel at others is just a projection of our own mind and is not based on reality. Most of us have, at some time, probably had a colleague we couldn't stand because we feel they're a terrible person, for example. Maybe you feel your colleague hated you from the first day you started your job, but that's only your view of it. What you perceive as their hatred towards you might simply be your colleague's fear of losing their job. Maybe this person admires you and sees that you're good at your work, but perceives you as a threat, and expresses that fear in negative looks or actions that you misinterpret. If you were to show them you're not interested in their position, and make them feel more secure, your relationship would quickly change. Soon you'd both be laughing at the rocky start you'd made together. Another instance could be when someone talks angrily to us a couple of times or says something unpleasant, and we immediately assume that this is a true reflection of the person. Next time, even before they speak, we feel sure they'll say something negative to us. The fact is that we don't know what's happening in that person's life. Maybe they'd just got divorced or lost a loved one the first time they were rude to us, and the second time they seemed angry, they'd just had a car accident. There are endless possible reasons for that person to have been angry, and their negative reaction to us was merely a projection of their inner feelings, and was not related to us at all. Maybe they have family problems, and feel stressed, frustrated and anxious most of the time. They needed to release that energy somewhere and you just happened to be the first person they encountered at the time. Having a bad day or week or year is no excuse for being rude to others and unleashing negativity onto them, but we should understand that, in most cases, the negative emotions the other person displays to us are not actually related to us. Instead of taking it personally, why don't we react with love and care just as we would if our kids came home from school feeling very angry. Again, we wouldn't think they were bad people, but would ask them what had happened at school to upset them, and we'd hug them and offer our advice. No doubt we should be more delicate with our colleagues, especially as some people don't like to reveal their problems to others. But just offering them an opportunity to confide and letting them know that you're ready to help could turn your relationship upside down. Instead of being a target for the person's anger, you could become a friend they can count on.

True, it isn't easy to treat other people in a similar manner to the way we treat our kids, but we should never dismiss the possibility that the other person is basically good and may simply have some problems that make them appear 'bad'. Developing this kind of awareness will be a stepping stone for us. Instead of assuming that every angry person you meet is bad; why not try to see things from their perspective? Simply ask them what's happening and whether you can help; show them kindness, care and love. If we all did this, we'd be able to eliminate at least half of the negativity and arguments from our lives. Wouldn't that be great?

ALL FOR ONE AND ONE FOR ALL

If you think you're too small to make a difference, try sleeping with a mosquito.

—Dalai Lama

'All for one and one for all' is the phrase best known from Alexandre Dumas' novel *The Three Musketeers*. It means that the three friends are united in supporting one another. We see this principle in many instances in our lives and it works regardless of the size of the group. The more we identify with the group, the stronger our support will be. The same principle can apply to two people, who could be a couple, for example; or to a group as big as our nation or even the whole world. The bigger the group, the harder it is for us to feel we're a valuable member; and the more difficult it is for us to be fully engaged. But then again, we can decide how much effort to put into it according to how dedicated we feel to the group or cause. The bigger the group, the more motivation we'll need, and the more understanding will be necessary in order to widen our horizons and see our role in the bigger picture. The more people who understand their significant role in the overall scheme, the easier it will be to achieve a better life for everyone.

IN YOUR FAMILY

Loving our family should be easy but there can sometimes be a lot of complications – that's why there are so many divorces. The main problem in these close relationships comes from our high expectations and from our disappointment if these are not met. Very often we ourselves fail to even mention our expectations to our partner and hope they will just read our mind. When they fail to do that, we accuse them of not understanding us. Sounds familiar? If we learned to communicate well with our partner and stopped expecting them to be responsible for our happiness, there'd be hardly any divorces, and maybe fewer marriages as well. We alone are responsible for our happiness – we need to look for it within ourselves and not in external things or from other people. Finding happiness within ourselves is too wide a subject to look at in any great detail in this book, but a study of Buddhist philosophy will help you understand how we are the masters of our own happiness – you'll find it very liberating.

The family is like a team – a group of people who all support each other no matter what. Even if the relationships are problematic, the family will come together in a crisis. In general, our family members all protect each other and care for one another, sharing the times of sadness and loss as well as the moments of joy and celebration. When we give our vows and promise to love our spouse for better or for worse, we voluntarily begin to form a kind of team that includes our partner's family, and that will extend with the arrival of kids. Nobody forced us to get married, although there may have been some family pressure or maybe there was a baby on the way. It was purely our decision and so we need to take the responsibility for it. We promised to love and take care of the family and that's what we should do. Often we forget that any marriage involves work, and if we do it well, we'll enjoy it. Advice is now available on 'team building', including techniques on how to strengthen relationships. We can't really expect to have a perfect relationship without effort from both sides.

The more love, understanding and kindness each member of the group brings, the closer the team members will be. It will be a case of 'all for one and one for all'. One or both of the parents will work to provide a good living for the family. They take care of their kids, feed them, clothe them, play with them, teach them and prepare them for life. The partners cherish one another – each demonstrating their love and encouraging the other to be a better person. Kids help their parents with different kinds of tasks around the house depending on their age, and show their love to the parents. Everyone is happy and grateful for what they have. Sounds too good to be true? It's actually possible. We need only look within ourselves for happiness before expecting everyone to act in the way we want them to act, and before we start blaming others. Let's not forget that it's our team and we should always want success for our team. It's tough if you feel you're the only one in the family trying to keep everything together, but you have to look at the situation carefully and be honest with yourself – others might view it differently. Do you give unconditional love to your family no matter how badly you think they behave? Do you blame them and attack them if they fail to respond well to you in return? By taking a step back and looking at the situation from a distance, you'll probably see that your love is not unconditional at all. It's difficult to admit it, but if you're completely honest with yourself, you'll understand that you're expecting something back in return. If you give your love to your husband, and expect him to help around the house, you're placing conditions on your love. On the other hand, if you give love to your wife, and expect her to cook for you and look after the kids every day, but she objects to this and you feel angry – you're placing conditions on your love. The same is true if you give your love to your kids and expect them to obey you and tidy their rooms – if they don't do it, you'll shout at them angrily – you're placing conditions on your love. We have to understand that everyone has their own perspective, and sees things in a different way. Even if we feel like we give and give and give our love and feel we're the only one putting any effort into the wellbeing of the family, other members might actually hold the same point of view concerning themselves. For example, if a wife who looks after the kids and cooks dinner every day asks her husband to help around the house and to spend more time with her, but he complains that he's tired, she'll feel like she's giving so much and getting nothing back. From her husband's point of view, he works hard to provide for his family and to allow his wife to spend her time at home with the family rather than working. He doesn't want to come home from work to find his wife complaining that he doesn't help her. Like her, he feels he gives so much but gets nothing back. So now we have a family that's supposed to work together as a team to be a happy family but both of the adults feel they're the only ones making the effort and giving their love, time and energy without being appreciated. Isn't it paradoxical that both parties feel they give so much love to the other person and at the same time the other person seems blind to this, and may even feel animosity in return? We may think we give a lot, but our giving is not really useful when it's in the wrong form. It needs some careful thought beforehand. It's like trying to feed an antelope with fish or meat and a tiger with grass and other vegetation. In *The Five Love Languages*, the book by Gary Chapman I mentioned earlier, the author clearly explains how to show love to people in a way that actually makes them feel they're loved.

In every team, whether it's a family, a sports team, a group of musicians or a work team, there'll always be disagreements and arguments, but it's our job to at least try and smooth things out or dispel the problems completely if possible. You simply need to remember that this is our team and we want our team to win. To achieve this goal we should listen to the other team members and discuss how we can best improve things for everyone to feel happy. We have to give what's *actually* needed rather than what we think might be needed – then we'll quickly see an improvement, and a more united and happier team or family. And who wouldn't want that? So let's be selfish and give to our family what they need so we can all be happy.

AT WORK

Team work is a phrase we hear a lot at work. These days more and more companies understand the importance of building a strong team, of making sure that every employee feels part of the group and feels that their input matters. If we plant the idea of: 'All for one and one for all' in the minds of everybody at work, the work itself will become much easier. It will be a team effort where everyone shares the same goal, and where we all support each other. If one person gets stuck in their task, the others step in to help. To create that type of atmosphere at work, the initiative has to come from the boss, or in the more progressive types of company, the 'boss' could be more like a leader than a manager or director.

The team leader both respects and inspires their crew, and values their opinions and ideas. He or she understands the importance of taking good care of their team because a happy employee will give 100 percent and will also work more creatively. If the troops fighting in a war are tired, hungry, wounded, and lacking in motivation, the soldiers will probably lose the battle. It's the same in business. We're fighting with our competitors every day. Maybe the ammunition is different, but we use the most powerful weapons we have to fight for our customers and capture our share of the market. If a company takes care of its employees, they'll respond well, and support the leader and the company in difficult times as well as making an extra effort when needed. Having a dedicated and loyal team is the dream of any employer, but only the ones that understand the importance of making their employees happy first can achieve this goal.

You're probably thinking 'yes, that sounds like a perfect working environment, but the place I work is nothing like that'. Maybe your boss is not a candidate for the 'Boss of the year' award, and your colleagues are the most annoying and selfish people you've ever known. It's a 'dog-eat-dog' situation, and it's like surviving in the jungle. Obviously when the boss has a positive attitude, it's much easier to create a productive and friendly working environment and good relationships between colleagues, but it's also possible to create something positive starting from the employees. Even if you hate your boss, you should do it for yourself. Wouldn't you want to be happier at work and feel a bit more positive about getting up to go to work in the morning? How much better it would be if you went to work in a good mood – you'd look forward to seeing your colleagues and telling them about some ideas you'd had in the evening or tell them a joke you'd heard? Even if your colleagues are 'impossible' to deal with, you can still start to change things. Don't forget that absolutely everybody has exactly the same wish – to be happy. The change will need some time, but remember that the motto 'All for one and one for all' can be reversed to 'One for all and all for one' so when *you* start the positive change, the others will see the benefits and follow. I can almost hear you say 'yes, it all sounds good, but my colleagues are terrible and it's impossible to change them'; but the truth is that it *is* possible, and the best way to defeat hate is with love. No one can say it's easy; but it's only as difficult as we think it is. Also, if we believe the reason for our unhappiness at work is due to our terrible and annoying colleagues, would we be happy if they were taken out of the picture? Do we feel happy when we arrive home from work because we're away from our colleagues? We have to understand that our terrible colleagues may not be as bad as they seem – it's our projection onto them that's negative. If we approach them with love and show a genuine interest in them they might respond well and turn out to be nice people. Also, if the atmosphere at work is unpleasant, there's a strong chance that some of your colleagues think that you're a difficult person, just as you view them; but you know that's not true. If it's not true for you, it may not be true for them either. If you still have any doubts, just try to imagine the following scenario: you woke up this morning having lost your memory, and you don't remember anything about the workplace except where it is and what your tasks are. It's not the same as the first day in a new job though because you'll not have the same fear or worry of not knowing what to do. You're already familiar with the place and the tasks, but you have to get to know the people. Go with an open mind and imagine that every single one of your colleagues is an interesting person and has their own fun side – try to get to know them and find out what makes them tick. You're an interesting and fun person, so why shouldn't they be the same? If you give them a few chances, they might really surprise you. The reason for giving them more than one chance is because they don't know about your 'memory loss', so they'll still see you as something of an adversary at first, and you'll need to be patient. When you start spreading love at work (and I don't mean sexual harassment), others will gradually follow your lead, and the change will happen. Once you and your colleagues are much happier at work, the work performance will improve and this will boost productivity. The boss's appreciation will help to motivate everyone to continue in the same spirit. When the boss is happy with the increasing profits, he or she might thank everyone with some nice gesture such a party or a bonus. Suddenly everyone will feel much happier at work, and slowly but surely the team will achieve even bigger and better goals.

What if your boss is greedy and inconsiderate, and simply pockets the increased revenues without understanding the reason and without appreciating the employees' efforts? You shouldn't worry about that. Remember that your goal was to be happy at work and get on with your colleagues as well as give yourself something to get up for in the morning. You have good reason to congratulate yourself now that you've helped to transform the atmosphere at work – now everyone is friendly and you feel a lot more enthusiastic about going to work in the morning! Keep in mind that even if the boss is a terrible tyrant, the team doesn't have to include him or her – your informal team could consist of only you and your colleagues. If the boss doesn't appreciate your work, no one is asking you to go the extra mile as you would for the best kind of boss, but you should do your job well to avoid feeling guilty. That way, you'll know you're doing the work you're paid to do, and you can also focus on maintaining a good relationship with all your colleagues. Most likely, you'll extend these personal interactions beyond the workplace to enjoy meals together after work, a bowling game or even a holiday.

As you see, it's definitely worth making the extra effort with your colleagues and giving them a few chances to respond well. You'll be much happier than you were before. Whether the initiative comes from the employer to the employees or vice versa, the team can put into practice the motto 'all for one and one for all'. You don't have to do it for your boss or for your colleagues at first, just do it for yourself. Soon, everyone will follow and enjoy the benefits.

ON A WORLD SCALE

It's much easier to understand the importance of the team and its common goals as well as giving the necessary support when we're looking at the small scale. The principles that apply to small groups, such as a couple, a group of friends, a family, or a sports or work team, can also apply on a larger scale such as our town, our country and our world. We need to understand that we're all connected, and just because we can't see the direct relationship between ourselves and the people on the other side of the world, doesn't mean the relationship doesn't exist.

We're all part of the same world and our actions all matter. True, we may appear insignificant on a world scale, where the population amounts to 7.5 billion people; we may feel powerless to change anything, but we're still a small part of it, and every part matters. Just as with any machine, if you remove one piece, the machine will not work properly. You might think that a machine can work without some of the parts, but it won't work as it should anymore. For example, let's take a fridge for an analogy and see how that would work. If we take out the plug, the fridge won't work because it needs an electricity supply to run. If there's a scratch on the side or on the door, the fridge would still work perfectly well as this wouldn't affect the performance or functionality at all. If it was for sale, the fridge would be considered as imperfect and sold at a discounted price. Some of the parts are important for functionality, some for aesthetics and others for convenience, but the fridge is only considered to be complete and worth the price if all the parts are there. Every single component is important, and has a certain function in the machine. Likewise, in communities of people, the bigger the group, the more difficult it is to see how one person can influence or change anything. But until we understand our common goal, we'll struggle with our small part in it.

As responsible citizens of the world, our main goals should include nurturing our planet and the natural environment rather than destroying it, and living happily together in peace. I know it sounds utopian because of all the bad people around us, but we're part of the group of those bad people and we have to work with what we've got. Fair enough, there are many people who do terrible things and set a bad example for the next generations in their family. There are also lots of greedy and angry people, who are destroying our planet as well as the lives of others for their own profit, but that doesn't mean we should just step aside and let them do it. It *is* difficult to see how we as individuals can change anything, but think about the compound effect. An action that seems very small and insignificant on its own can become something magnificent when added to other actions. To look at the compound effect in reverse, we all know how our salary tends to disappear very quickly – even though we don't splash out on anything big, it just seems to dwindle away regardless. It's all the small daily expenses that add up and make our seemingly substantial salary vanish so quickly.

A more positive example would be a brick. A single brick isn't very useful, unless we're attacked on the street and use it in self-defence. But when we join a lot of bricks together we can build our family home in a structure where every single brick matters. Taking away one brick would result in a hole in the wall.

We all have an important role to play in the world, so it's good if we understand that. We can then help to initiate the necessary changes or join some of the movements that are already trying to improve our wellbeing. If you drop a piece of rubbish on the street, it may seem like a tiny unimportant thing that has no real effect on anything, but let's not forget that there are 7.5 billion people here, and if everyone drops rubbish on the streets, the world will become one big rubbish dump. These days we understand the importance of recycling more than we did a few years ago, when people didn't realise that the small amount of rubbish they produced at home would make any difference. Again, when we look at the global population, it means a lot of rubbish. We need to act as a team in which everyone has an important role to play. When we think about any action we're about to take, any purchase we're about to make or certain things we might want to use, which don't seem important on such a small scale – multiply it by 7.5 billion and think again! If you use plastic cutlery for picnics or special events, for example, think again! You'll avoid adding further to the piles of plastic waste, and save yourself some money at the same time!

Imagine if we all had to live in a dump, breathing polluted air, drinking contaminated water, eating food full of chemicals and suffering from a terminal disease as well as constantly arguing and fighting with everyone; and either feeling angry or miserable all the time. A lot of people do actually live like that, although no one ever plans for things to go that way. And it's not only about saving the planet – it's also about the interactions and relationships among people, about positivity and happy feelings. The more we give from our side the more we'll benefit; so if we feel reluctant to act, let's do it anyway for our own sakes. Please don't panic, nobody is asking you to become a full-time environmentalist or a relationship expert who knows how to get along with literally everyone. Although we need to take it slowly, and shouldn't expect immediate results, we do need at the same time to face the fact that change starts from within us and we need to actively encourage it. Let's think about ourselves and how we'll benefit from living in a clean environment, from nice clean beaches when we go on holiday, from breathing clean air and eating healthy food. Our change of heart and positive actions will also help us feel safer and happier; it'll bring us more fulfilling relationships and help us to be more at peace with ourselves.

We actually belong to a group called 'The Whole World', and yes, maybe it's slightly bigger than our usual groups, but the principle 'All for one and one for all' still applies. The sooner we understand the important consequences of all the actions and choices we make every day, no matter how small, the sooner we'll head towards saving our planet and improving our quality of life. If we all could see the bigger picture, it would make so much more sense – the more of us that give to the world, the more we'll all get back from it and the faster the positive change will happen. We're already on our way; we just need to press down on the accelerator a bit harder to move more quickly towards our common goal.

FIND THE PURPOSE IN SHARING TO MAKE THE CHANGE

Compassion is the radicalism of our time.

—Dalai Lama

In our present age of technology we can connect with the other side of the world in a matter of seconds. At the click of a button; we can immediately get to know the news from anywhere in the world; and not only does information travel faster than before, but we can also travel from one place to another in a much shorter time. But even so, we're actually less connected with each other than before. Although we have all the possibilities that technology provides, we barely use it or we use it in the wrong way and for the wrong reasons, wasting all the potential opportunities. Technology gives us an incredible amount of power, and what we can achieve is almost limitless, but we're so afraid of change that we don't use the power we have to encourage it to happen. Most people play it safe instead, and share cute puppy or kitten pictures, which is understandable. But the point is that we have so much potential power that we can achieve anything if we use it in the right way. Of course, everyone needs to collaborate, and it'll take time, but big breakthroughs never happen overnight.

DISCONNECTION IN CONNECTION

It seems somewhat paradoxical that we have friends on social media from all over the world, but we don't know our own next door neighbours. How many of your neighbours do you actually know? That means not only knowing what they look like (sometimes we don't even know that), but also knowing their names; what they do for living and what they like doing to unwind. What are their interests and what are their worries; what makes them tick and what makes them happy?

In this high-tech age, the easy connections that are available with the rest of the world are incredible. Just by using a smart-phone and an internet connection, we can see live streaming videos with very good quality visuals and sound from another part of the world. We can have a conference call involving people from different countries or even continents, so that no one needs to travel to attend the meeting, and decisions can be made there and then with the participation of all the various branch managers. Now we can easily visit friends abroad or travel across the world in a matter of days. Imagine how long it would take us to travel those distances by horse and carriage? It would've taken us around two weeks to travel from Berlin to Vienna just a couple of centuries ago, and now it takes less than 1½ hours on the plane. Even if we add a few more hours in calculating the time getting to and from the airport, it's still pretty amazing.

We're connected through countless platforms, social media, blogs, forums, chats, dating websites and apps. We're connected to our friends, family, acquaintances, colleagues, people we met when travelling, and even people we've never actually met. It's true; we have contacts on our apps who we hardly know. We may even start thinking how nice that person is, but for all we know the person might not be who they appear to be at all. But that's another matter. Let's focus instead on the online contacts we have actually met but don't know much about. There was a funny joke, when one guy had the wrong birthday date set up on his social media profile and everyone congratulated him on his fake birthday. The climax of this story came when he got a message from his dad wishing him a happy birthday. How many of our friends' and family members' birthdays do we actually know, and how often do we just rely on the notifications from social media? Do we have friends on social media who haven't set up their birthday on their profile, so we don't get any notification? Do we even realise that we've never seen a birthday notification for the five years we've known them or do we notice after a year passes and ask them for the date? Do we think we don't need to directly tell our friends about our news because we've already posted it online, and so we just assume they've seen it?

Most of us have at least one friend who can't put their phone down even when they're in the company of others for dinner, drinks and catching up. You might also witness disconnection by observing the group of people on the next table – all four of them are busy with their phones instead of chatting and having a laugh together. You may also have seen a couple out for the evening, who are both engrossed in online activities on their phones rather than in each other. Instead of strengthening their connection by showing attention and affection to each other and asking about how their partner's day went, they are quite disconnected from each other. We all know parents who give their children a phone or tablet to occupy them instead of playing with them or teaching them something useful. We've all also seen groups of teenagers taking selfies, and having little or nothing to say to each other even though they claim to be friends. Sometimes I feel that my own generation, born before the advent of the World Wide Web, was the last generation who had a real childhood, having played with our friends, spending a lot of time playing outside and using our imagination to come up with many different activities.

Now, not only are children robbed of their childhood, but adults are robbed of their ability to connect with real people every day. For myself, having read a book a while ago about relationships, I picked up a few basic tips about how we should smile at people and make eye contact to initiate a connection with a stranger, I decided to try it out. I'd moved to London a few months previously, and needed to make some new friends. It was late spring and the weather was starting to get warmer every day – the sun was out, and I could feel good in a nice dress and show some of my skin after being wrapped up in a winter coat and scarf, and wearing big boots. It seemed the perfect time for the experiment. I remember feeling upbeat and energised – I was sure the task would be very straightforward – all I had to do was smile, look the other person in the eye, and maybe say 'Hi'. The nice dress would help, I thought. I walked along the street with a big smile on my face and looked at the people I passed every day on my way to work. After continuing to do this for a few days, I realised that it was actually very difficult. And it wasn't anything about my ability to smile or chat with people, the issue was that I could only see the top of everyone's head because they were all looking down at their phones as they walked. Maybe it wasn't actually everyone, but around 80 percent of the people I passed. It gave me quite a shock. The sad thing was less about the difficulty of making new friends as the disappointment at seeing so few people smiling. Smiles are very catching – if someone smiles at us in the street, we immediately smile back, and then we smile at someone else and bring them a small moment of happiness, and so on and so forth.

This is not to suggest that we should dump all technology and return to the Stone Age. Technology is a great thing that helps us with a lot of tasks in our daily life, but shouldn't we prioritize the more important things in life and give these our time and attention accordingly? Technology should assist us in making life easier and in helping us to free up time so we can focus on other things, but many of us become slaves to technology and allow it to control us completely. It can become a form of addiction – once we've tried it we can't stop using it. If you don't believe that's true, just try living without your phone for a week. How many of us could even get through one day? Many people would find it unbearable. Our attachment to our phones has reached the point where dropping our phone and shattering the screen is much worse for us than the death of a distant relative. Isn't it sad that a gadget means more to us than a human life? Of course, gadgets are cool, but they should serve us and not the other way around.

We need to get our priorities right and understand that the internet and the connections it offers us are great and useful, but what really matters are the connections and interactions between human beings in the real world rather than in the virtual one. And we should do it for selfish reasons. If we do all our communicating online, we'll never even learn how to communicate in real life or we'll lose the skills we do have. Yes, we can go online to use a dating site, for example, or use an app to find someone, but sooner or later we'll need to meet that person face-to-face. If we don't practice our communication skills in the real world, the first date with someone will most likely be the last one as well. Likewise, we can use websites to find a job, but we'll need to attend a face-to-face job interview or real-time video chat and use our communication and interpersonal skills again – otherwise, we'll have a lot of interviews and no job offers. How about having a laugh and getting into a good mood? Yes, we can watch a funny video and even share it online, but the joy will last only while we watch the video and maybe for a few minutes afterwards. On the other hand, if we meet up with some friends, have a nice chat and a laugh, we'll still feel energised and uplifted the next day, and even a year later it'll put a smile on our face when we remember that great evening with friends. We just need to differentiate between online connections and real-life ones, and understand the role that each should play in our life.

POSSIBILITIES AND POTENTIAL IN CONNECTION

Technology itself is great, but slavery to technology obviously isn't. Technology gives us so many opportunities we didn't have before and saves us a lot of time as well. We can do our shopping online, for example, and save ourselves at least half of the day as well as saving our energy as we don't need to go around various shops or carry heavy bags – the goods are delivered straight to our door instead. We can spend the time we saved on something more productive, such as watching TV or playing computer games – I'm joking of course! We could save some time on shopping at the weekend, and spend it with family and friends; we could give more attention to our loved ones; read an interesting book; do some exercise; go for a walk in the park or start working on the project we always wanted to do. What an amazing time we can have with only a little effort, filling our day with joy and happy feelings.

If you've just booked your holidays online, you'll obviously be looking forward to the trip away, and feel excited. We'll also have saved ourselves some time by booking online instead of spending half a day going to various travel agents and looking through their brochures (something the future generations won't know anything about). It obviously takes time to research and choose holidays online as well, but at least we save maybe a couple of hours in the travelling time needed otherwise. It's our choice whether we use these two hours for a positive improvement, for pleasant experiences with the people around us or whether we just disappear into the virtual world and kill our time without experiencing any positive emotions.

If we can perceive technology for what it actually is – a tool to help us with our tasks – we could use it according to its purpose and function to gain all the benefits from it. We have all kinds of potential opportunities, but unfortunately we're wasting them. The people who wake up and start to grasp these opportunities first will benefit the most; so again, we should do this for selfish reasons – we obviously don't want to lose out. With the help of technology, people who start using the free time they've saved can work on the projects they've always wanted to start so their good ideas can come to life and bring income to the owner of the idea. The people who wake up first will probably earn more money because they'll have a bigger market of customers that will blindly follow, still in their virtual consumerism world. Those who wake up first and start teaching others have a better chance of gaining respect as well as a good reputation. Even if a lot of people wake up after them, they'll be followers, and although they may become teachers as well, the ones who started first have more potential to have a stronger influence, and will be respected gurus for many others. We all want to be rich and famous to some extent, so it should be extremely motivating for us to wake up and start using the time technology has saved us in a positive way and for selfish reasons.

And it's not only about our potential to earn more money. Working on a project we've always wanted to do or learning a new skill or language will give us a tremendous feeling of achievement – we'll feel proud of ourselves and have fewer regrets at the end of our life for not doing the things we wanted to do. We'll spend our spare time doing something we love, which will give us fulfilment and lots of joy. We'll learn something new; we'll improve ourselves and will become a more interesting person. And when I suggest you use the time technology has saved you in a positive way, I don't necessarily mean taking a couple of days off for doing things you like, but I mean that any spare time is better than nothing. If we use the technology to help us save as little as 15 minutes a day, it could be enough for the first steps to a happier life. If you've always wanted to learn French, for instance, but never had time to do so, why not use these 15 minutes to learn 10 new words in French. As people use only about 600 words in everyday life, you'll need only 60 days to learn that many words. Allow a bit more time for the basic grammar rules, and you could learn a new language in 3 months by spending only 15 minutes a day. Even if it takes a year, you can still learn a new language instead of just thinking about it. Imagine what we could achieve if we used technology to help us utilise our spare time – learning something as we commute to work instead of playing computer games, for example. Maybe some of us can't be bothered to actively study, but we could also learn something from watching certain videos and tutorials or by listening to audiobooks. Everyone wants to be a cooler and more interesting person, so why not use the potential you have to improve yourself?

We have the possibility of using technology to connect with the people we love and enhance our relationships as well. Instead of playing games on our phones during the commute to work we could be writing an email to a friend we haven't seen for a long time. And for those of us who travel on the underground where there's no signal, we can still type the text of an email while we're underground and send the message once the connection is available again. If we catch ourselves asking why we should write an email to a friend when he or she hasn't written to us, don't forget we're doing it for selfish reasons – it will bring back nice memories of the things we experienced together and it will cheer us up as well as helping us feel closer to our friend just by thinking about them. And who doesn't want to feel good and smile all day? Besides if we keep good relationships with our friends, we'll be invited to visit them for dinner or a party and could have more good times and positive experiences.

We can also use technology to connect with our parents. How many of us are too busy to call them, and always find excuses for not keeping in touch. Maybe it was more difficult before when we needed access to a landline phone and had to dedicate time to sit there and talk to them. These days it's so easy though – we can just put on our headphones and talk to them while cooking, cleaning the house or tidying up the car. There's a very moving video on YouTube ('Edeka 2015 Christmas Commercial') about an old man who had unsuccessfully tried to gather all his kids for Christmas dinner every year – they were always too busy or too wrapped up in their own lives to go, so he would have Christmas dinner on his own. Then one day, all his kids received a message saying that their dad had died, and they felt devastated. They all dropped what they were doing, took time off work and travelled together with their families to pay their last respects to their dad and granddad. When they arrived at his house, all feeling very sad, they found the dinner table set for a meal and there was dad very much alive and waiting to greet them. They were all confused until he said: 'How else could I have brought you all together?' There was probably not one person watching this video who could hold back their tears. As the saying goes: 'We don't know what we have until it's gone.' Even if we usually try to avoid communicating with our parents these days because we find them annoying, and constantly wanting to talk to us, we need to remember that regularly keeping in touch is for our own benefit as much as for theirs. The moment we lose them we'll regret how we neglected them and how we missed so many opportunities for contact.

Giving our time to people who we love doesn't mean we're giving something away. We actually gain more than we give by doing so because when we give love, we receive the same in return. We also benefit later in our life when we are free of regrets, and can enjoy a lot of positive emotions and happy moments along the way.

Using our time to develop an idea or a project we want to do can also give us unbelievable amount of joy and fulfilment. Even if we don't make much money out of it, we'll still be much happier than if we'd spent that time on the couch watching TV – we'll definitely learn something in the process of doing something we love. By using technology to save time, we can spend that time on something more meaningful and we should do this for selfish reasons because it'll be very beneficial for us.

SIX DEGREES OF SEPARATION

You've probably heard the term 'six degrees of separation'. Introduced by Frigyes Karinthy in 1929, it refers to the idea that any two individuals can usually be connected by a maximum of six steps. In the chain of the 'friend of a friend', we're just six steps away from any given person in the world, no matter whether it's a Hollywood star, the president of any country or a farmer in a remote location.

In some cases, the distance between two individuals might be more than six connections and reports showed the maximum degree of separation was 12 in 2009, but the average number was five or six. Considering there are 7.5 billion people in the world, even 12 is a very small number of steps between any two people. With the growth in social media users, the distance is becoming smaller and smaller with averages of just 4.74 in 2011 and 3.57 in 2016. It's difficult to grasp the full implications of this theory that states we're all interconnected with everyone and the distances between us are very small, even though it's hard to imagine yourself connected to someone in a remote village on the other side of the world. It's incredible to realise how closely we're all linked, and how our 'friend of a friend' network can reach the furthest point in the world.

We tend to protect the people we're connected to, and to discriminate between the people we know and those we don't. The ones we know are important to us, and we generally don't care much about the others who are strangers. Most of us would make an effort to help people from our circle but would usually dismiss requests from people in the street. Not many people see how we're all connected. Imagine how everything could change if we paid more attention to this theory of six degrees of separation, and broadened our understanding of its implications. We could stop the negative effects that come from feeling disconnected from others, and we could use the true power of our connectivity to improve our relationships with others and even with the Earth itself.

We mistakenly believe that only we ourselves are important. Our definition of 'we' is the group of people closest to us and those we view as similar or the 'same' as us. Our attitude is rather like that of the supporters of a football team who think that their team is the best, and that the opposing team and their supporters are all idiots. Likewise, the members of a certain political party think they are right and their opponents are wrong. A group of teenagers may think they are the cool kids and look down on the others as the 'losers' and 'nerds'. If we could look at the whole world as one though, and understand how we're all connected, would we deliberately hurt the other person who is essentially part of 'our' group? Would the teenager bully his or her best friends' little sister or brother? Would a mother let her neighbours' kids die from starvation? Wouldn't you give some food to your former classmate who's now homeless? Maybe we should ask ourselves questions like these when someone needs help or when we have bad intentions towards others. Could it be that we're somehow connected to that person? Just imagine the situation where you do something careless or inconsiderate to someone at work or school – maybe you bully them or make fun of them, or you simply ignore them because you think they're not as good as you are. You later meet someone very nice, and fall in love – you feel very happy and can't imagine life without them. When you're invited to meet your lover's family, it turns out that the person you'd mistreated was a member of their family. That wouldn't go down very well, and there's a strong chance that your lover will take the side of their family member rather than yours – you might even lose this person. And unless you're heartless, you'll not feel very good in this situation either.

177

We can't predict where or when such situations will arise, but we can very easily prevent them by treating everyone with respect and with the understanding that we're all connected. If we keep that thought in our minds and hearts, we'll avoid such awkward situations – if we meet that 'friend of a friend', we'll have treated them with respect and may even have helped them in one way or another so they'll be thrilled to see us again and they'll greet us with a big smile and an open heart. Don't you want to be welcomed everywhere you go? This can happen once you start the change yourself.

We tend to put people in different boxes and often think that our box is 'the good one' or 'the right one' and the rest of them are wrong, weird or even bad. But the boxes are not real. We created them in our minds or with the help of the media or another influential group. At the same time, the labels we put on people are imaginary – we could easily re-label them as being members of our group if we looked from a different perspective. The video on YouTube 'Stop putting people in boxes...after all we're all the same' is very inspiring. It shows how incorrect we are in labelling people and dividing ourselves into groups. By using different criteria we'll find we have more in common than we thought. In the video people were put into different boxes according to various stigmas, and then people were asked to step out if they met the criteria stated; such as having been bullied at school, if they're step-parents, if they've saved a life; if they're in love; if they're lonely and many other different things we can have in common. People from different boxes were stepping out to form a new group according to the things they had in common. The video shows that we're not as different as we think we are. The simplest and most universal feature is 'people who want to be happy and free from problems'. Literally every single living being on earth without exception would fall into this category. Maybe the definition of happiness would differ between individuals, but we all still want to be happy. So if we all have the same goal to be happy and free from suffering, why do we think that we're different from anyone else and even feel hatred towards people who are 'different' from us?

We need to open our eyes and start seeing the truth for what it is. We're all connected and we're not so different from each other after all. Another very touching video on YouTube 'Momondo – The DNA Journey' shows how imaginary the differences are. The researchers tested the DNA of volunteers to trace their ancestry. When a British man, who was sure that he and his parents and grandparents were really

British, was asked which nationality he disliked most, he said 'German'. He added that for him, Britain was the greatest nation in the world. Similarly a Kurdish girl said she didn't want to have anything in common with the Turks. The results revealed that the man who thought he was 100 percent British was only 30 percent British and also had 5 percent of German blood in him. All of the volunteers had mixed blood and nobody belonged 100 percent to the nationality they identified themselves with. If we all knew where our ancestors came from, and how diverse we really are, there'd be no place for extremism or for so much hatred in the world towards others. Even if the science behind this experiment is not entirely accurate, and the percentages given for each region or origin of our ancestry deviates from the actual percentage, it doesn't change the fact that our ancestors come from various places. Whether the result's 40% British, 25% French, 5% Egyptian and 30% Turkish; or 35% British, 30% French, 10% Egyptian and 25% Turkish; the message is still the same – the person has British, French, Egyptian and Turkish blood. And where before they might have had negative feelings towards one of these nationalities, they would now look at it a little bit differently, wouldn't they? How can we hate something that is a part of ourselves?

We need to open up our minds to the idea that we're all interconnected through the 'friend of a friend'. We have various things in common, and our diverse ancestry shows that we all belong to the same world, and have many things that bind us together. We're much closer to each other than we think we are, and if we open up our minds and hearts, we can make the world a better place to live in. Don't you want to live in a world where everyone smiles at each other and respects each other, and where people are more compassionate and ready to help one another? Don't you want to live in a world where neighbours get along well and enjoy good times together; where governments work for the people of their country and for justice instead of their own material gain; where there's no hatred between races or nations and where everyone works, both individually and collectively, for the benefit of everyone else? That world would be an amazing place to live in, wouldn't it? Because we want to live in a world like that we should start the change from the one place where we really have the power to do it – from our mind.

THE POWER OF SHARING

Looking at the six degrees of separation, we've now established that we're more connected than we thought, and so it will be easier to see and contemplate how much power sharing can actually bring. When we share things, the message goes beyond the closest people in our circle to reach others at the other side of the world. If you remember the chapter 'Pay it Forward', where we looked at the positive effect of each person helping three others, the maths will work in the same way with those who received the message we shared, and it will grow exponentially.

We all know some videos or stories that went viral in a matter of days, and the whole world was talking about them. Those examples perfectly illustrate the power of sharing. Without sharing there would be no viral videos; no viral stories and, as a matter of fact, no stories at all. If everyone kept everything interesting that was worth sharing to themselves, there'd be no videos or articles made in the first place so there'd simply be nothing to share on social media. A journalist who asks the questions and writes the story is the first point of sharing the message. The story they heard from the source, which they may have investigated more thoroughly, becomes the final form of the message they want to share with the world. The person filming someone rescuing a trapped animal, and posting it on social media; is also the first point of sharing as they produced the message to share with the world. Life coaches who create inspirational videos to share a positive message with the world are the first point of sharing. If no one shared with the rest of the world, we'd all be living in the dark; and literally. Scientists are among the people who create the messages worth sharing, on inventions, for example. If Thomas Edison hadn't shared his invention of the long-lasting electric bulb, we would literally be in the dark.

This equation of sharing the message has two main components that are co-independent. The first is made up of the people who create the message worth sharing and put it out for others to see. The second component comprises those who share the message and create the possibility for it to reach the whole world. Both parts are essential for achieving the positive effect. If we have only someone creating a message but no one else to share it, the information will remain stored in one person's mind and will have no power. On the other hand, if we gather a hundred million people who agree to share a message with others, but no one actually supplies the message, there'll simply be nothing to share, and again, nothing will be achieved. Obviously, if we gather a hundred million people in one place, it will be one hell of a party and a very powerful crowd, but technically, a message about the party will still need to be shared to gain that huge power. One component can exist without the other, but in order to attain the power of sharing and make a positive impact on the whole world with our message, both components need to be in place.

The power of sharing then; consists of those who create a message and the others who share it. Another important aspect is the power and effectiveness of the message itself, and this is strongly influenced by the individual approach of the person who originates the message. Obviously, it will vary from one person to another. An exceptional message will have huge sharing power. A weak message, on the other hand, will have weak sharing power if any at all. Also, each of us will find different messages important or interesting. While many of us may join others to support certain causes, for example, and that's how groups for certain interests are formed, no two individuals will have identical interests and views on all aspects of life. The message itself will have sharing power among those interested in the subject. The exceptional message can capture the attention of people who have neutral views on the subject though, and sway them towards supporting the message and giving it more sharing power. This kind of remarkable message may even help to change someone's mind about a subject. To change someone's negative view towards a topic with just one message is probably impossible – but it can be the first step in moving towards a positive change.

The better the message, the more sharing power it has and the more chances of becoming viral and reaching the whole world. A variety of approaches can achieve this effect, and these usually trigger one of the basic emotions or feelings of fear, anger, sadness, joy, disgust, surprise, trust or anticipation. Although some of these emotions are positive and some are negative, in some cases, the message could aim to achieve a positive outcome by triggering negative emotions such as fear or sadness. Certain social topics can be presented with quite a negative background, and the aim is to produce a positive effect by raising awareness on the issue in question and encouraging more and more people to act in a positive way to address the problem. The most successful messages usually trigger surprise and anticipation – the strong emotional reaction makes these messages stay in people's minds and have a big effect. These types of messages will spread widely because people want others to experience the same positive reaction they just had themselves. The message can come purely from the heart with a strong feeling of love to bring joy and happiness – it can often cause emotions so intense that it brings tears of joy. We're naturally far more inclined to share any message that reaches the depths of our hearts.

CHOOSE WHAT WE SHARE

These days there are more and more inspirational messages that touch us to the core and have a positive effect on us. These messages help to change lives and motivate people to achieve their highest potential. But unfortunately, many others go viral that are not so positive, to say the least. You've probably seen 'The Backpack Challenge' on YouTube, for example. The goal of this challenge is for a schoolchild to try and run through the group of school friends who stand on both sides of the path and throw their backpacks at the runner to try and knock him or her down. And let's keep in mind that these backpacks, full of text books, are heavy, and so could easily hurt the friend who's running. It seems we moved on from filming our friends who've hurt themselves or have fallen accidentally, to videos where we deliberately hurt our friends. It's sad if hundreds of thousands of people find that fun. Shouldn't we love and help our friends instead of hurting them and laughing at them? Maybe true values and love are out of fashion and we can only hope that this is part of a cycle and that the former values will come back into fashion again, and that we'll learn from our mistakes.

Another interesting phenomenon is 'The Mannequin Challenge'. This one involves filming someone in an informal setting while they are frozen in a particular pose. Where have we seen it before – the image of someone standing very still? It looks like a photograph. Although I sometimes wonder why they don't just take a photo instead, I have to admit that some of the videos / photos are really creative and look pretty cool. Doing something that develops creativity and doesn't hurt anyone in the process is much better than 'The Backpack Challenge'. But even so, it has no real positive effect on the quality of our lives and does nothing to inspire future generations.

Members of this generation nearly all have a big wish to be famous, regardless of whether they have any talent, and wish to find fame with very little effort and without giving any commitment to a goal. They want to have their '15 minutes of fame', and social media and YouTube make it easy. Anyone can become an instant star by getting noticed and getting as many hits and likes as possible. The problem is that such fast fame has no solid base such as talent or skill, and so it's very short-lived. The more people who strive to be famous in this way, the shorter their span of fame will be – it can only last until another 'big thing' comes the next day or even in the next hour. It's very dangerous to associate our happiness and fulfilment with the amount of attention we get from strangers – it means we're placing our happiness in the hands of others, and we therefore have no control over it. When people get their '15 minutes of fame' by chance, they feel a huge rush of positive emotions as all the attention makes them happy and even ecstatic. But once the moment passes, they feel empty and disappointed as they realise it doesn't last long. They get hooked on that feeling just as with a drug addiction, and want more and more of it. Unfortunately, just as with drugs, these people can experience bad as well as good 'trips'. It's usually impossible to repeat the first brief success, and the victim ends up hooked on the 'fame drug' and the bad trips it brings, making them depressed. On the other side of things, the people who become famous for their talent or skill feel happy knowing they worked really hard to get where they are now, and for the recognition they now receive for their hard-earned achievements. The appreciation of their talent or skill encourages them to work even harder to get better at what they do, so that the rest of the world can enjoy the fruits of their efforts. This type of fame is likely to last longer than 15 minutes, but the fame and attention has it pitfalls even when talent and skill are involved – there's a lot of pressure to be in the spotlight all the time – and this is especially difficult for a young person to cope with before their personality is fully developed.

Fame doesn't have to be worldwide. Instead of being a star on TV or YouTube, where you might get millions of shares and have your '15 minutes of fame', why not be a celebrity in your own local community? By doing something meaningful, you can share your kindness and win the respect and admiration of others. This type of fame is much more solid, and can even last a lifetime. Depending on what we do, we might become famous even beyond our own community – our dedication and kindness can take us there, and we'll feel much happier about the process than about the result of being famous. We could visit our elderly neighbour once a week for a cup of tea, for example, to keep them company for a while – there are a lot of lonely old people in the world. Maybe we could do their shopping every week, and if we have more than one elderly neighbour in our area, we could even perform this small service for a few neighbours at the same time. This type of action and demonstration of goodwill will definitely cheer people up as well as filling your heart with satisfaction and other incredible feelings. By showing such an example, we can inspire others to do the same thing. Maybe our story will appear in the news, and we'll get attention and recognition for what we do. There are even bigger benefits than this because actions such as these also help to strengthen communities. If some strange character is loitering around our car or watching our house to see when we leave it, for instance, and may be planning to burgle, normally the neighbours wouldn't pay much attention to it. Even if they noticed, they'd be scared to do anything about it, thinking it's not their business to get involved. If we've developed a good relationship with a neighbour by helping them out from time to time, they'll feel respect and appreciation towards us. What do you think they'd do then? Even though we'd helped them without any expectation of reward, the neighbour will have a strong desire to protect us and protect our property if they can. You'd be surprised at how heroically an elderly neighbour can act – and their strong connection with us will mean they'd see it just like protecting something of their own. Obviously it doesn't mean our neighbours have a duty to watch and protect our house, but the point is that a strong sense of community widens the focus of the individual members and means they'll act in the interest and wellbeing of all the members.

Many people say they don't have the time, the money or the wish to help others, but everyone has time to share the videos and posts that interest them. Even the busiest person on earth still finds time to go on social media every day, so why not use that time more productively? Instead of sharing things like 'The Backpack Challenge' or 'The Mannequin Challenge', we could share something more meaningful like a positive inspiring quote or a motivational video; we could sign and share a petition for a good cause; share a video that shows an act of kindness or share anything else that teaches us something good and can have a positive effect on the future. These days there are plenty of positive things to share. People often turn to Eastern philosophy for wisdom and to rediscover the ancient truths about life and happiness, which are still relevant today even though life is so different than it was two or three thousand years ago. People are also becoming more active when it comes to supporting good causes, and social media helps immensely. We don't have to be organisers, but at least we can be a part of the process and help to spread the message that supports a good cause.

We always have a choice in life and it's always up to us what we do. Sometimes it's not easy to make decisions, and sometimes it might seem that we're not in control of our decisions at all, but the final choice is still ours. Choosing what to share on social media seems a very easy choice to make, but we often forget that our share counts, and the amount of pointless messages we share is frightening. It's obvious that sharing positive and meaningful messages is beneficial, whereas sharing negative and meaningless messages is not. For some reason there are a lot of meaningless messages that go viral, and meaningful ones that get overlooked. But we all know that there's an eternal fight between good and evil – we just need to hope that the good will triumph as it does in fairy tales. And if we open our eyes, we'll see that we live in the best times when there are endless possibilities of sharing things with the rest of the world without even leaving our own home. If we realise that we can contribute to the big change that will lead us to a better future and make the world a more beautiful place to live in, we wouldn't hesitate for a second the next time we share something, and the choice will be obvious to us – we'll always choose the positive message.

TIME NEEDED FOR A CHANGE

In the age of instant gratification when we expect instant results for literally everything in our lives, we need to acquire a little patience. No big change happens overnight. Maybe sometimes it might seem that some big change just came out of nowhere, but you'll find that a long process has always led to it, involving lots of work and dedication. Every big change was the result of long hours, weeks, months or even years of devoted effort in moving towards that goal. Although the breaking point is often mistaken for overnight success, the measurable results that stun the world are usually the result of a lot of hard work.

Even in everyday life, progress never happens as quickly as we'd like. It's true that if you have long hair and want to change to have a short hairstyle, the change will be sudden and dramatic – the result will probably surprise other people as well as yourself. But then if you want to grow it back, it'll take a year or more for your hair to reach its former length, and we can't speed up this process. Similarly, to achieve many other changes we also need to have the patience to slowly move towards our goal.

If we're building a house for our family, we can't expect it to be finished in a week. Just obtaining planning permission will take more than six weeks for a start. After that, looking for an architect and some good builders, sourcing materials, making decisions in the process, getting agreements with neighbours and the building process itself will also take a long time. Of course some building methods are quicker that others, but we still need to have realistic expectations of how long it'll take to build a house. And then, we need to prepare for the possibility of quite significant delays, because construction work often involves unforeseen factors and delays. Whatever the task, we can only do our best to make sure the process runs as smoothly as possible, and after that we need to 'prepare for the worst and hope for the best', as they say. So long as we understand the process and let it run in its own way, we'll start seeing results before too long. One day the building of the house will be completed, and we can move into our new home and enjoy every corner of it; we can feel pleased that the building process is over and admire the final result.

Learning something new takes time as well. Do you know anyone who sat behind the wheel of a car for the first time and was able to drive a car with manual transmission proficiently? Do you know anyone who started speaking a foreign language without any exposure to it or without any lessons or study? Do you know any of famous and talented musicians who became a great professional as soon as they picked up an instrument without thousands of hours of practice beforehand? Obviously some people learn their skills more quickly than others, and some have an innate ability for certain things, but no matter how talented a person is; they still need time to learn and practice a new skill.

If the process of changing seemingly small things in life takes time, we can't expect the big changes in the world to happen overnight, especially when we talk about, people's mindsets, beliefs and prejudices as well as dogmas in society and the habits that have been ingrained throughout many generations. History shows us that any change is possible and there's nothing more constant in life than change itself, but even the smallest change requires time. The bigger the change, the more time it needs. If we want to change a habit, it takes at least 21 days to break the habit and replace it with new behaviour. Some habits require more time, and others require less. Let's say the electricity supply to our house gets cut off and we know there's no electricity in the house; but we're creatures of habit and every time we come into a room we still press on the switch. And we keep doing that for the rest of the day even though there's still no electricity.

Knowing the facts about the change and consciously understanding the situation doesn't stop us from being driven by our old habits. We just keep forgetting that there's no electricity because our habits override our mental awareness.

Therefore, when activist groups are trying to change the world for the better, they not only have to inform people about the facts of the issue and the benefits everyone will have, but they also have to break old habits and replace them with new ones. When it comes to changing big matters in the world, an additional issue is the huge amount of money involved as big corporations lobby governments to support their business that is damaging the environment. It all continues for the sake of bigger profits though, even though the Earth and many of the living beings upon it are suffering as a result. And it's not only climate change we're talking about here, but there are also other issues such as gun control in the U.S. It's clear that change is needed when there's one massacre after another – it shocks the whole country every time as many people lose their loved ones. Gun control seems like a natural solution after so many deaths from firearms. It would mean banning automatic weapons and allowing people to have only small guns for self-protection as well as implementing more in-depth background and mental health checks before issuing firearms licences. Licence holders would also have to attend an extended mandatory course on gun use. Unfortunately, a change in the law is slow to come because of the huge sums of money involved in the business. Sooner or later the change will come. It seemed that the tobacco business was infallible and very powerful with its vast profits, but the laws related to the advertising and sale of tobacco products are now quite strict in many countries. Some countries in the world have banned advertising for alcoholic beverages as well. Let's not forget that there used to be slavery, so we know that change for the better is possible, and probably even inevitable. We just need to work towards it systematically and continually.

Just as science helps us to predict and control natural and economic processes in the world, we can also predict and control how an individual or a group of individuals will act in certain situations. We can calculate things with a high level of accuracy, but at this moment we often can't control the greed which makes us blind to the truth and hurts others as well as ourselves. Before we can make a big change in the world, we need to start with ourselves. We need to understand that even a limitless amount of money will not bring us the happiness we seek. We need to look for that within ourselves. We might think that money brings happiness, but there are a lot of very rich and miserable people in the world with broken families and relationships, drug problems and with a constant fear of being robbed or kidnapped that makes them hire security staff and bodyguards. Imagine how you'd feel if you had all the stuff you'd dreamt about, but felt lonely and scared as a drug addict without any real friends and with no one you could trust. If we learn how to control our obsession with money and all the stuff we buy, and start to see that it's not the source of happiness, we'll stop grasping it and expecting bigger amounts of money to make us happy. Money itself is not a bad thing; it's actually beneficial because it allows us to help others as well as ourselves. It is the greed for more and more money, and the belief that money is the source of happiness that is bad. And if we alter the way we use our money, a lot of people would be happier. If we can abandon our greed, we'll teach and bring up our kids accordingly, and they'll bring up their children in the same way as well. We'd be only one or two generations away from a perfect world. The big change that's needed in the world would be much easier if many more people could live a happy life without greed. Money, which often stands in the way of good causes due to the profits made from harmful types of business, would lose its power over people.

The only thing we can be certain of is that everything in life will change. Our role can be important in the grand scheme of things, so we need to make the right choices for the benefit of the whole world as well as for ourselves. In the state the world is in at the moment, and considering the mindset of the people, it seems that change is far away, but it really all depends on each and every one of us. Everything little counts, and if we all put our effort and resources together, we can create a new positive power, and our kindness and selflessness can change the world. But in another sense, our actions would be selfish because every one of us wants to be happy and free from problems, so we would be doing all that for ourselves as well.

CONCLUSION

Be the change that you want to see in the world.
—Mahatma Gandhi

Being selfish and giving to others gives us a very positive perspective on the world we live in. The selfish reasons for giving are not actually negative at all because your happiness at sharing with others is for the benefit of all. The main goal of this book was to make you aware of how giving to others is actually beneficial to you, and of how much you gain by giving away. Hopefully this book has helped to open your eyes a little wider and broaden your views as well as showing you how everything in the world is connected, and how the actions of every one of us are important. If we all join forces – each of us making small positive changes and all pulling together in the same direction, this joint force will soon become very strong. There's no pressure though – nobody expects you to change right away. Just keep an open mind to the possibility that you can be part of a bigger move to help create a better world.

You don't have to become Mother Teresa II – we all know that the sequels are never good. You can help the whole world by becoming someone unique – become bigger and better than anyone else in the field! If you don't have such grand plans, do what you're comfortable with. Any small change for the good is much better than nothing. It's better to act on a small scale than to stagnate. Start slowly by watching the videos on YouTube mentioned in this book, let them deeply touch your heart and be inspired. Experience that warm feeling inside – that's how love and compassion feel. Don't try to change rapidly, choose one type of action, and gradually increase the good things you give to others or to the natural environment. And remember, when you give to others, you actually give more to yourself, so the process is suddenly in your own interest.

Changing habits is not an easy process. It is absolutely doable and possible, but it requires a bit of an effort on our part at the very beginning. The good thing about it is that we just need to replace our old habits with new ones. And, as we already know, the new habit will soon become part of us, and then we won't have to strain ourselves to do it after some time, it will become natural to us and we won't even notice we're doing it. It's easier when there's some kind of incentive for this new habit. We've known for a long time, for example, that we can reduce the amount of plastic bags we use by reusing old shopping bags. Many people just get new plastic bags every time they shop and then let them pile up in the kitchen. When U.K. shops started charging 5p per plastic bag, many people started taking their own reusable shopping bags with them. Although 5p is a small amount, this charge gave most people the incentive to change their habits. Britain's plastic bags usage has dropped by 85 percent since this charge was introduced. But when we think about it, why do we wait to be pushed to make a positive change? Why don't we set ourselves a goal and give ourselves a small incentive to follow it through? Hopefully this book has given you a few ideas and examples of how we can all make a shift, change our direction and start moving towards a better world without breaking the bank or forcing ourselves to do things we would hate. Start small and gradually pick up speed once you're comfortable in your new seat, and remember – it's beneficial for you!

To motivate yourself you can think about the positive effects your actions will have for you. You'll feel much happier, and your spirit will be uplifted. It's always nice to see a smile on people's faces and it's good to know that you contributed to it. You'll feel proud of yourself for doing the right thing. You'll be respected and admired by others and become more popular. You might even become a real-life hero! You'll create a flow of positive energy that will increase the positive things in your life. As the saying goes: 'What goes around, comes around.' Whether you believe that at the end of your life you'll get the last judgment, or you believe in karma and future lives, it's our actions and attitude to others that will matter the most in both scenarios in influencing what happens to us after this life comes to an end. Nobody wants to suffer in any way, so it's in our own interest to accumulate as much virtuous merit as we can. Even if you don't believe there's anything more after the end of this life, and believe that we just get eaten by worms in the ground after we die, the principle of 'What goes around, comes around' is valid in this life because all our actions have consequences for us sooner or later. When we give to others we actually give to ourselves, we broaden our views, expand our circle of friends and extend our knowledge as well as improving our health, happiness and quality of life. Unless you give away all you have and leave yourself destitute or get addicted to the Helper's High, there are no negative effects from giving to others, only very positive ones. Everything we do should be done wisely, and giving away everything you own is not wise. You need to look up the side effects and risks of Helper's High, to be aware of the symptoms and avoid any negative effects. The rule of thumb – everything is good in moderation. Don't overstrain yourself helping others to the point where you'll be the one who needs help. Open up your heart and mind to others, but always take care of yourself first. Remember, helping others is for your own benefit as well – it should give you happiness and improve your life – so it's in your interest to do it wisely. And last, but not least, the motivation for giving is actually to improve your home, in the broadest sense of the word. And, yes, I mean the planet Earth. You, your kids and their kids will have a much better life in the future if we all take care of our planet now. We want them to enjoy fresh, unpolluted, air; clean beaches and a clean sea as well as having the chance to observe some of the beautiful and fascinating animals in the world. We also want them to live in a safe environment on dry land with fewer and less devastating natural disasters, and avoiding the kind of future shown in the science-fiction movie *Waterworld* (1995), where after the polar ice caps melt, most of the globe is underwater. We don't just want to survive; we all want to live happy, safe and fulfilling lives. Each of us has a part to play in ensuring that we can have such a world.

Changing the world starts with just a shift in your awareness as you begin to see the bigger picture and understand how even the seemingly small actions done by one person, lead to big results when we add together all the people who are doing their bit. Everything each of us does counts and we want to make sure we move in the right direction towards a better world. And if you still don't feel like you're ready to help others and the planet for your own benefit, at least don't do any harm.

In a gentle way, you can shake the world.

—Mahatma Gandhi

You can find links to Youtube videos mentioned in
this book and much more at:
www.joylovegoodwill.com